CW01337792

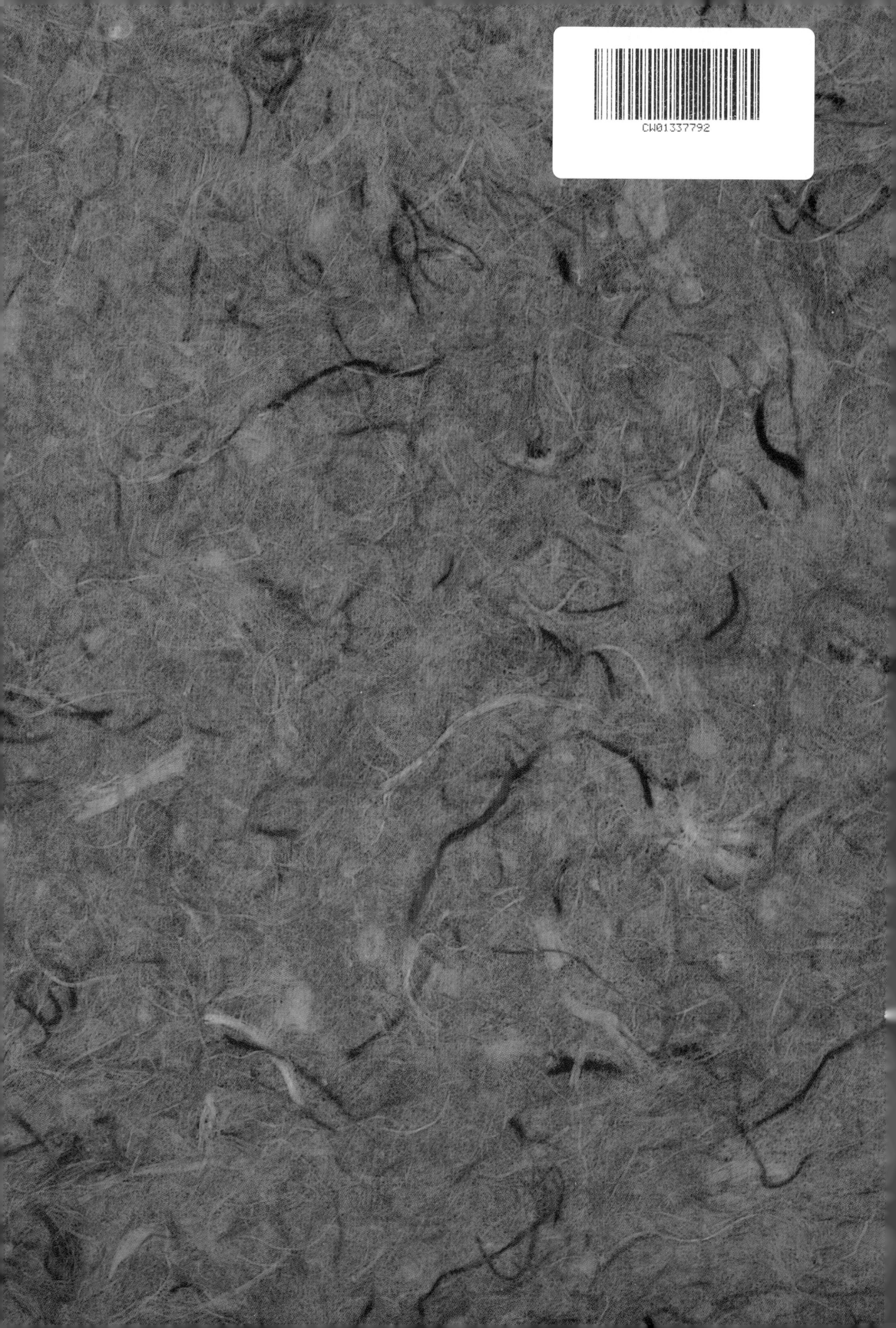

THE BOOK OF
YOGA

This book was first Published and Distributed in Great Britain in 2002
by Tara Patel

ISBN 1 904046

© Tara Patel
Publication date: 1st May 2002

All rights reserved. No part of this publication may be reproduced, stored in
a retrieval system, or transmitted in any form or by any means, electronic,
mechanical, photocopying, recording or otherwise, without the prior
permission in writing of the author.

Whilst great care has been taken in the compilation of this book,
it is regretted that no responsibility can be taken for the use,
or consequences of the use, of the information and advice contained herein.

Editor: Muriel Halsall

Photographer: Bhupendra Patel

Typeset and designed by Priory Publications,
238 Smallfield Road, Horley, Surrey RH6 9LT

Printed by Uday Bhojani at VSSU Graphics

Be a Light

"Be a light, be a light,
O ye faithful be a light.
whether in the yogi's cave,
or to your family a slave,
be a light, be a light,
shining radiant and bright,
where He needs ye, go with light,
be a light, to chase all night,
whether in the home.
or all alone, He waits for thee,
not on a throne.
but in thy star, within thy sight,
amongst the darkened by a light . . ."

Forwards

This book arises from the many years, which the author has spent practising and teaching yoga to all kinds and conditions of people. As in all the best teacher/pupil relationships, the benefits have been reciprocal. Pupils and fellow-travellers on the eight-fold path of yoga have been inspired by Tara's teaching and by her example. This book leads us gently but firmly in the practise and principles of yoga. Those whose way of life is already based on these principles will find them reinforced; those who are putting a tentative step on the pathway will find inspiration and encouragement. It is the heartfelt wish of the author that this book will lead many more people to continue to gain the blessings, the inspiration, and the immense benefits that are there for every body and every soul to share.

My first impression of the book is that it is simple and well presented, with its soft, warm, and relaxing colours. Generally, yoga's advanced postures are seen as being difficult to hold, but the ease with which Tara holds these postures defies that notion. The postures appear firm, yet soft, denoting disciplined effort put in by the author. There is a neatness and relaxed poise in these asanas that symbolise the correct manner in which they should be taken.

I have no hesitation in endorsing Tara's vision of yoga as a most precious gift to humankind. I heartily recommend this book as a valuable guide to all those on the royal road of yoga.

— *Dr. Pankaj Naram (Director of the Ayushakti Ayurveda Health Centre, Mumbai, India)*
6th February 2002

Blessed are those who grow up with a sincere yoga-teaching parent, blessed am I to have witnessed such unflinching dedication and discipline towards the path of yoga, from my mother, Tara Patel. This book was not born out of the desire to sell copies, nor even to spread the message of yoga; Tara made this book out of the sheer love of yoga. I cannot recall a single day in the last few years where Tara's mind, heart, and soul have not been immersed in the completion of this book; it is her life's work, and the spirit with which she has imbued these pages will be felt by all who are fortunate enough to discern this book's priceless quality.

— *Mr. Neil Patel (The Chi Kri School of Yoga, London, UK)*
6th February 2002

The Book of
YOGA

I OFFER THIS BOOK to all who, through the practice of yoga, would like to live in harmony with the laws of nature.

The Book of Yoga illustrates 96 Yoga asana (postures), pranayama, bandha, mudra and satkriya. The photographs are arranged alongside the relevant text for ease of reference. There is an introductory article on yoga and an explanation of each of the eight limbs of ashtanga.

Sanskrit has 50 letters in its alphabet and it is very difficult to translate exactly Sanskrit texts into English. It is possible, therefore, that in this book there may be some discrepancies.

The masculine gender has generally been used in order to avoid the constant repetition of 'he or she' and 'his or her'. Yoga is for all, irrespective of gender, race, creed or politics. In Indian Spirituality, God is worshipped in both male and female forms. The scientific terms and explanations have been simplified as far as possible.

I hope this book inspires its readers to practise the time-tested science of yoga and make it their way of life to attain health, happiness and peace for all mankind.

Work and Relax with Yoga

ॐ GURU ॐ

By the revelation of the law of karma
You show me my dharma.
Freeing me from the bondage of maya
You show me nirvana.

ॐ YOGA ॐ

Preface

The Thrill, Love, Joy and Peace I feel when I practise or teach Yoga cannot be adequately expressed in words. If it was possible to do so and convey the extraordinary feelings experienced, then it would be easy to convince people to make Yoga their way of life.

Yoga is a great spiritual experience in which science and art are fused into a beautiful and harmonious whole. It is through Yoga that one can reach a stage where one experiences union with Self.

Many times, either when practising or teaching, I have paused to pay humble reverence to this great art. Yoga classes have given me strength and shown me the way to overcome my fears and doubts.

I await for what is yet to come my way from this fathomless ocean. Has my past karma been so good that I have been led, almost accidentally to tread the path of this great Yogic experience? Surely somebody up there was and is most lovingly looking after me.

Like all people, I experience many of life's ups and downs. I dread to think how, without yoga, I would cope and deal with life.

This book is offered as a guide to Yoga but it is no substitute for personal tuition by a practising qualified Yoga teacher.

I hope that the inspiration and guidance you receive from this book, will make your life happy and peaceful.

Acknowledgements

To God, for without his grace neither I nor this book would exist. For His help and guidance in developing my body and mind coordination through Indian Dancing leading to the path of Yoga.

To my beloved guru Paramahansa Yogananda, whose teachings enabled me to begin to lead this life wisely.

To my dear father, whose simple and upright life was an example and a blessing for a growing child and which has been a continuous inspiration in everything I do.

To my mother, who was always there for me and who, through simple and loving life, taught me great lessons of life.

To Rakesh, my dear son for invaluable support and understanding at all times and for his generous financial and moral support.

To my dear son Neil, a spiritual friend and a young yogi, for sharing this life's drama with me, for practising and spreading Yoga, and for all the help with typing, photographs, videos and audios.

To Kirit, my dear husband and friend, for all the strength, co-operation, financial help and encouragement in writing this book and during all the years I conducted yoga classes at home.

To my dear friends, Muriel Halsall, Kapoorbhai Shah, and the late Charles Brien, for proof-reading, clarifying, and making suggestions.

To my brother-in-law, K.J. Thakrar, who was a yoga practitioner, for introducing me to yoga.

To Shama and Mahesh for helping with the Sanskrit texts.

To Mahesh, Jo Cohen and Neil for their photographs.

To Bhupendrabhai, Kirit, Neil and Vimal, for patiently taking the photographs for hours on end.

To my yoga friends in various classes, for their love which kept me teaching at my best in spite of having health problems and domestic difficulties. Thanks for coming trustingly, lovingly and sincerely to the classes. Thanks for taking me further in my yog-sadhana. Thanks for sincere help in compiling this book.

To the late Dr Chandrasekhar Thakkar (of Sindh pharmacy in Bombay), a teacher of yoga and ayurveda.

To Sushilaben Patenkar of Bombay for personal tuition on yoga cleansing kriyas, pranayamas and bandhas and mudras.

To Babubhai Patel of Bombay for free tuition.

To the late Philip Jones for teaching me pranayamas, bandhas and mudras in my early days with yoga.

To the writings and study lessons, by my beloved guru Paramahansa Yogananda, and the books by Vishnudevananda, Dr C Thakkar, B K S Iyengar, Shri Shivananda, Shri Satyananda and other yogis.

To Gloria and Ken of Kenneth Copeland Ministries, Texas and other Christian ministries for bringing home to me the invaluable message of yoga through the Holy Bible and the life of Lord Jesus Christ.

Contents

Yoga	9
Yama and Niyama	12
Asana	21
Pranayama	138
Pratyahara	147
Dharana	148
Dhyana	149
Samadhi	151
Bandha and Mudra	152
Nadis and Chakras	157
Sat Karma	160
Yoga Therapy	169
Glossary	173

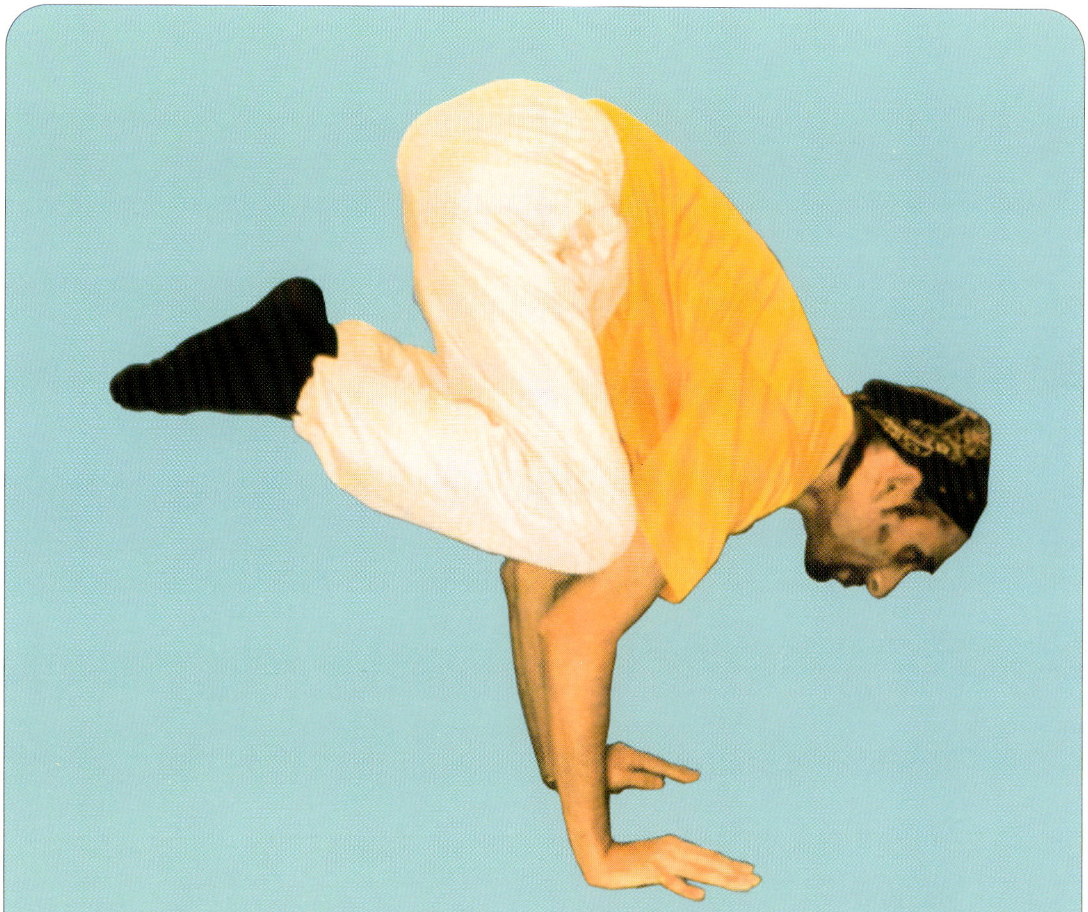

Yoga

Introduction to Yoga means Introduction to happiness.

Because man's true nature is Joy, he cannot help but continuously crave for happiness in all he does. Man's ego, which is deeply identified with the falsity of maya (delusion), makes him seek this happiness outside himself rather than from within. The meeting of the self and spirit in yoga fulfils man's deep desire.

The word 'Yoga' is derived from the sanskrit word 'Yog'. It means to methodically and skilfully cause and experience joy in the merging of Jiva (Atman) and Shiva (Paramatman). It means to create and enjoy the scientific union of the body, mind and soul. In simple words, yoga is a conscious and controlled undoing of the wrong done to oneself in the past in order to re-establish one's lost true 'Nature'.

Yoga helps to create good health. Good health means physical and mental strength and well-being, abundant energy, clarity of thoughts, mental efficiency, zest and love for life and peace of mind. It can lead to the joyous fulfilment of one's dream. It can help to create material and spiritual wealth and success. It is also a crucial factor in attaining spiritual perfection.

We all have the potential for good health and yoga teaches us that it is fostered by positive attitudes and actions. Our negative emotions, thoughts and actions present an obstacle to this power within us. We have the ability to be happy or unhappy at any given moment in all circumstances.

Health and happiness are affected by the state of mind. One can have all the material wealth, physical youth and comforts of life and still be unhappy. On the other hand, one could have none of the above and still be full of life. A retired pensioner with health and financial problems who remains calm, strong and happy amidst his trials, is better off in life than a strong-looking young millionaire who is stressed out and walks glum-faced. A positive, willing, contented and cheerful attitude awakens nurturing energy in one's life. The greater the zest and the will, the better the flow and the power of the energy. In contrast, a dissatisfied, grudging attitude to life leads to dis-ease in the self; a lack of sustaining energy and of true happiness. When inner life currents are persistently abused by negative mental and emotional movements in one's self, the life force suffocates, not having suitable positive outlets. Disturbances manifest in the workings of the body and mind. The body's immune system shows signs of disease and fatigue. The weakest part of the body gradually starts malfunctioning, resulting in illness.

Yoga teaches that man is responsible for his own health and happiness. We can choose to be healthy and happy, or diseased and depressed. The Law of Karma declares that we are creators of our own destiny.

If our intention is to put health and happiness first in our lives, we must arrange our priorities accordingly. We must follow a balanced and healthy diet, do physical exercises, think and act positively and be regular and disciplined in our daily life. We should keep balance between work and leisure, discriminate between good and bad, keep good company and read books which would help us to lead a decent and meaningful life. In the sixth Chapter of the Bhagavad Gita, Krishna says (vi:16-17) "Yoga takes away the sorrows of those who are moderate in their eating and recreation, moderate in all their actions, moderate alike in sleep and wakefulness."

Sometimes, it seems that most of us spend our youth, health and strength to earn wealth, fame and other material success without proper care for our body or mind and then in illness and/or in old age, we spend our greedily accumulated wealth to try to regain lost health.

Yoga is a discipline and a science that unites body, mind and soul through its balanced systematic, skilful process that keeps all levels of our being in peak condition. Through its balanced physical and mental exercise programme, breath control, good diet, body and mind detoxifying techniques, relaxation, visualisation, its philosophy, spiritual counsel and meditation, yoga can free us from all suffering. There is no problem too big or too complex for yoga not to be of help.

Most people begin their yog-sadhana (discipline) from a general hatha yoga class. When somebody says they are going to a yoga class, they generally mean that they are attending a session of hatha yoga where they are taught physical postures called asana, and breathing exercises known as pranayama; yog-nidra (relaxation techniques) and some simple light meditations.

Asana are the most well-known part of yoga. We are all conscious of our physical being and so the practice of asana has an immediate appeal. A baby sucking its thumb and playing with its hands and feet shows the extreme awareness that a human being has with his body right from birth. Our bodies fall naturally, without conscious effort, into one or other postures. The physical postures we adopt, the attitudes, thoughts, feelings and gestures we express, reveal the state of our consciousness. When we adopt yoga postures, we consciously initiate beneficial changes in the body and mind, and in life in general.

Hatha yoga is a gentle process of self-development. Gradually but surely the ashtanga yoga helps one's male and female mind to work together. As they work in harmony, the body, breath and the mind become strong, supple and calm. Problems and their solutions are seen more clearly. Through yoga, we are empowered to deal constructively with our self created sufferings, and to avoid causing further tensions. To a faithful practitioner, hatha yoga is a beginning that leads to the most purposeful life. It is not surprising that people of all ages, races, colours and creeds all over the world are drawn to this great eternal science of life.

Hatha means 'strong determination' – an unbending, uncompromising will. Hatha yoga through asana, pranayama, sat-kriya, yog-nidra and light meditations is a psycho-physical training programme.

'Ha' stands for the sun and 'Tha' stands for the moon. 'Ha' is the shining (Creating) and 'Tha' is the reflected (created) light of the sun. A yogi is a Creating and created energy (light) of Divinity.

Raja yoga is the science of self realization. Absorption of mind is attained step by step through advanced pranayama and meditation techniques, reuniting the soul with Spirit.

Absorption of mind attained through deep concentration by the continuous chanting of Pranava (the soul liberating OM sound), aloud to begin with, then whispering and finally finishing in silence to unite self with silent Self is called Laya or Linga yoga. Linga means to link or unite.

The samsara (creation) in which we find ourselves is a sea of maya (delusion). Yoga is the boat and the scriptures such as the 'Bhagavad Gita' and the 'Holy Bible' are manuals instructing us how to avoid the pitfalls of maya, and how to safely and quickly paddle to the Source of joy. The collective strength of all the yogis, as they merge self into the Self, gives birth to a whole new era, a mighty 'Golden Age'. In India, the scriptures call such an age 'Satyuga'. It is the age of Aquarius, that we can thus foresee being born through yoga. How can we afford to miss this boat?

Paramatman (Spirit) is Bliss, Love, Peace, Wisdom and Joy. We are mostly restless, anxious, nervous, angry, resentful, selfish – a bundle of numerous imperfections. To free ourselves from these imperfections and achieve union with Spirit, we must intelligently exercise discipline and self control.

Buddha said: "Unshakeable deliverance of the mind is the sole purpose of this life." Yoga trains body and mind to regain and to retain control. Strength comes from control. Useless ideas and practices are shed. Yoga exercises lead to a peaceful and contented life. When the positive change is steadfast for a significant period of time, an all-round stable personality – a yogi – is born.

In yoga sutra, Patanjali – a great Indian sage, devised a system of yoga called 'ashtanga'. Ashta means eight and anga means limbs. These eight limbs are yama, niyama, asana, pranayama, pratyahara, dharana, dhyana and samadhi. Angas (limbs) correlate with the development of koshas (layers), (see Yoga Therapy chapter). Some liken angas of yoga to the eight steps of a ladder with yama as the first step to the other World, whereas others feel that Ananda (bliss) is the hub of the wheel with each anga being a spoke. In order to accelerate his evolution, a yogi continuously tries to tie layers and angas neatly together in order to remain at the ananda (bliss) centre all the time. In the final stage of his evolution, a yogi is said to be in the world, but not of it – in the 'Nirbhikalpa' samadhi.

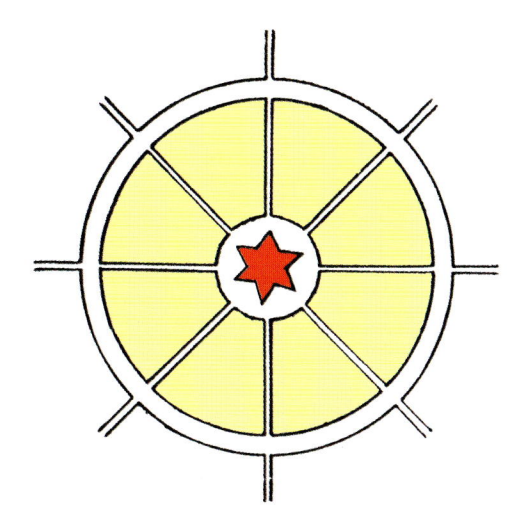

यम नियम

Yama and Niyama

A yogi diligently applies the principles of yama and niyama in his life, to make progress on the path of Self-Realisation..

The practice of yama and niyama helps in self-mastery. Yama are the rules of morality. They require firm determination to abstain from doing wrong. Niyama are resolutions to control and guide actions of the body and mind to do right.

There are five yamas and five niyamas.

Yamas are:

1	**Ahimsa**	non-violence
2	**Asteya**	abstain from stealing
3	**Satya**	truth
4	**Aparigraha**	non-covetousness
5	**Brahmacharya**	moral life

Niyamas are:

1	**Saucha**	purity in body, mind and words
2	**Santosha**	contentment
3	**Tapa**	righteousness
4	**Swadhyaya**	study of the Self
5	**Ishwar-Pranidhana**	total faith in God

The implementation of yama and niyama can be compared to putting one's house in order. The best thing to do is to get rid of all the unwanted and useless items and then make the home comfortable. Uprooting bad samskaras (habits) is yama and developing good habits is niyama. Unless we get rid of bad habits, we cannot enjoy the fruits of good habits.

While we concentrate on eradicating bad habits we should also at the same time make a sincere and diligent effort to cultivate good habits. We must not get caught in a situation where we find that the more we pressurise ourselves to get rid of bad habits, the more entrenched they become.

Daily meditation, swadhyaya, positive thinking, good company, inspirational books, observance of yama and niyama greatly help with the cultivation of good habits.

Yama and niyama are inter-connected. For example, Saucha – purity of body and mind – when sincerely observed will fulfil certain aspects of ahimsa, asteya, satya, aparigrapha, santosha, brahmacharya, tapa and so on. The observance of tapa includes ahimsa, asteya, saucha, santosha etc.

Most people have a tendency to see faults and shortcomings in other people and not in themselves. Yoga helps us to recognise our shortcomings and the ways of dealing with them. Perfection is the nature of soul, and one will never be truly satisfied unless one's faults are eradicated.

If one does not practise these principles then various problems arise and one suffers. Life becomes uncomfortable and difficult. In many cases suffering has led people to embark on spiritual life.

Many people begin yoga sadhana by practising two simple bahir (outer) angas of ashtanga – asana and pranayama. Yoga works holistically. The practice of yama and niyama helps the practice of other ashtanga and their practice strengthens observance of yama and niyama which in turn leads one to a life in harmony with God and nature.

Swadhyaya teaches us that if we first study our habits and tendencies, then we are more likely to be successful in dealing with them. It is not wise to attempt to correct faults without their measured assessment. Sometimes a problem may become worse if unnecessary pressure is applied. When unsure, it is best to give oneself time and space and not allow the ego to take over. One should be resolute on one's intentions to practise 'Yama and Niyama'.

It is better to live by the difficult principles of yama and niyama for lasting peace and harmony than by sense pleasures which give temporary satisfaction, but which are forever in conflict with the Self.

Ahimsa

A means no

Himsa means violence

Ahimsa means non-violence

Violence does not only mean acts of physical assault and killing. It also includes anger, revenge and hurting people with thoughts and words. In Sanskrit, the mother of all languages, 'vi' means 'against the grain'. Anything that disturbs or goes against nature and anything that causes pain to any body, mind or heart is himsa.

It is important to remember that violence harms the perpetrator as much as the recipient. Physical violence which has origins in one's inner-self, is an abuse of one's soul. It also affects the victim's inner energies. When violence becomes habitual, the defence mechanisms of the victim and the violator are weakened, resulting in eventual manifestations of disease.

We have a choice of dealing with our shortcomings and those of others. We are free to act righteously as dictated by our conscience and to reject the temptation for wrong action. In Deut. 30 v 19, we read "I call heaven and earth to record this day against you, that I have set before you life and death, blessing and cursing: therefore choose life, that both thou and thy seed may live."

Egoistic man feels powerful when he can exercise control over his surroundings and companions. Any threat to this control results in resentment, anger, anxiety, tension or bitterness which may lead to a violent reaction in words and deeds. The reaction may be ruthless or thoughtless. This often results in a breakdown of the body's defences. Mental and physical illnesses could ensue. According to the Hindu Scripture – 'Bhagavad Gita', anger obscures man's wise nature and paralyses his will. The stress, resentment and violent thoughts cause immeasurable damage to body, mind and soul.

The knowledge of the Self brings peace and love, diffuses anger and stops one from committing acts of violence.

Yoga teaches us the right way to physical and mental health, happiness and peace. We are able to develop the strength and stability required to live a truly sensible and virtuous life. We realise that it is love and not himsa that is the key to a successful and happy life.

Ego makes one seek sensual and material pleasures. One struggles to maintain the misguided desires by aggression, evil deeds, thoughts, ruthless competition, anxiety and a distorted view of one's nature. The result is suffering, deprivation and unhappiness.

Alternatively, one may master the ego and through love, discrimination and compassion seek truth and peace for lasting happiness.

A true warrior will always fight for the truth. He recognizes the errors and seeks to correct them. To forgive and to love in all circumstances is his motto.

Asteya

A means no

Steya means to steal.

Ignorance is the root cause of excessive craving for pleasure. Intense liking for anything leads to attachment. Attachment results in steya. Acts of steya include stealing, manipulating situations and people, deliberately misinterpreting information, gossiping about others and abusing trust etc.

The acquisition of wealth, status, health and happiness by dishonest means, deprives others of what is rightfully theirs, and affects their happiness and security. A dishonest person may sometimes cause irreparable damage and suffering to others. His acts are against the dictates of God within and they take him further away from happiness. The web of maya clouds the wise nature and distorts the vision.

Continuous dishonest behaviour causes bad samskaras (character) and corrodes one's consciousness. Bad karmas are created for our present and future lives.

As desires multiply, one gets involved in more acts of steya. A thief believes his acts are normal and that others also do what he does. The stress, greed, fear and guilt, created by his acts rob him of peace of mind and happiness. He may selfishly and sometimes ruthlessly lead innocent people to commit evil acts, giving rise to undesirable aspects of society in which robbery, violence, rape etc. are common and there is little caring and sharing.

Misfortunes are a blessing in disguise for such a person. He begins to question his motives for the evil acts and the selfish behaviour. He learns the lessons of life, becomes introspective and develops spiritually .For physical and mental health, happiness and peace, we must correctly establish our priorities. This may help others to do the same.

All our imperfections originate from ego. Yoga is a powerful way to understand and guide our energies for a wholesome life. It is a simple and practical way to happiness.

Satya

Satya means truth

Mahatma Gandhi said 'Satya is God and God is Satya'. Truth is universal. It is pure and simple. It is the core of reality and is the very essence behind everything. It is eternal. "It is".

Truth brings peace. Man's greed prevents him from following the path of truth. A busy man is prevented from distinguishing between truth and falsehood by the selfish ego. Unless he chooses to live by the principles which unify with the Self rather than by the easy rules which provide temporary relief, he will forever be in conflict with the self and remain unfulfilled.

To tread the path of truth requires honesty. The follower of this path states his opinions and ideas pleasantly and clearly. He recognises the right of others to contradict his opinions. He accepts the outcome without grieving or cheering. He is always happy since he expects nothing from others. He is loving and forgiving. He is always at peace.

Truth means to act righteously at all times, to discern right from wrong and to take the right course even when it is difficult.

The common definition of this yama is 'not to tell lies'. Lies are told for various reasons. A liar is not bothered by the harm he inflicts on others. Lying affects one's character and no-one escapes the consequence of lying. The law of Karma says, 'Whatsoever a man soweth that shall he also reap.' (Gal. 6:7).

Truth and love must go hand in hand. When Truth is painful it should be stated with love.

Aparigraha

Parigraha means to covet, to hoard

When one identifies solely with the body, one is deluded into believing that true happiness lies in the gratification of the senses. One forgets that material possessions give only transitory comfort and pleasure. The desire to acquire unnecessarily, is often a reaction to deep insecurity and unhappiness caused by low self-esteem.

It is possible that inordinate cravings for 'things' may lead some people to immoral and dishonest acts to acquire them. Covetous people may ask and accept favours, gifts, services and charity or they may steal or commit other evil acts putting their and other people's lives in jeopardy.

Acquiring and hoarding unnecessarily can become a habit and the priorities of life can get distorted. The distinction between wants and needs is lost and man ends up with more of what he fancies and less of what he needs. There is so much junk in his surroundings, body and mind. He eats more than his stomach can handle, covets or collects more money than needed and this affects his health and peace of mind. His ignorance keeps him attached to the body and he forgets the soul.

Unfortunately, the false image of success based on material power, impresses and influences other ignorant people around him. This leads to societies and nations which selfishly and with impunity exploit other societies and nations in the name of development, modernisation and progress. When man gets caught in greed, covetousness and self-destruction, his defences against disease are weakened.

Jesus says in Matt. Ch.6, V. 19-21, "Lay not up for yourselves treasures upon earth, where moth and rust doth corrupt, and where thieves break through and steal; But lay up for yourselves treasures in heaven, where neither moth nor rust doth corrupt and where thieves do not break through nor steal; For where your treasure is, there will your heart be also."

Aparigraha means limiting one's desires. It also means self-respect, inner strength and trust in one's ability to acquire honestly what is needed when it is needed. Without these qualities, one is poor and weak, no matter how rich one is materially and how strong one is physically.

Awareness of the true priorities enables one to lead a simple and morally rich life.

Brahmacharya

Brahma means the all pervading Spirit, Creator
Acharya means character, conduct

So that he may know Brahma, a yogi disciplines himself to develop a God-centred existence. He examines his motives and controls his thoughts, words and deeds.

He may be predominantly a raja yogi, jnana yogi, karma yogi or bhakta yogi.

"Each soul is potentially Divine. The goal is to manifest this Divinity within, by controlling Nature – internal and external. Do this either by work or worship, by psychic control or philosophy, by one or more, or all of these and be free."
(*By Swami Vivekananda*)

1. Raja Yoga
With the help of advanced scientific pranayamas, bandhas, mudras and meditation, a raja yogi awakens the kundalini power and channels it to the highest centre. In this way he transforms his consciousness.

2. Jnana Yoga
Through pranayama, meditations, swadhyaya, and right living a jnani trains himself to seek divinity in life. He serves God's creation impartially with cheerfulness, honesty and sincerity. He renounces the rewards of his service. He is constantly on guard against maya's insidious charms. He knows its complex and powerful nature and with the shrewd fingers of wisdom, he meticulously applies the rules of right living.

3. Karma Yoga
Family life, is the most fertile ground in which to practise karma yoga. A karma yogi spiritualises his duties and his activities.

Parenthood teaches us the highest form of human love and sacrifice. In social and family life, a karma yogi enthusiastically, unconditionally and happily gives love and service. He shows faith in himself and in God. He carries out tasks, however humble, to the best of his abilities. Although the end result is important to him, his aim is to experience happiness and fulfilment through the process of serving others.

A married couple following the traditions of old India, see sex as natural and pure and for procreation only. They feel responsible for their act. They see God as the Creator of all life. To them sex is a small part of true love. Control comes naturally as they see marriage as a union of two souls put together to teach each other to love unconditionally. Today the word love is too often confused with lust. In a healthy state, sexual desire is to free one from lust. Unhealthy sexual desires and activities keep man's energy and consciousness bonded to the lower base of life. They lead one to fruitless squandering of energy, infatuations and restlessness etc. They entail a great loss of vital, creative life-force. On the other hand, a forceful suppression of sexual desires is also harmful.

In the Bhagavad Gita (Edwin Arnold 11:47) Lord Krishna teaches, "Thou hast the right to perform thy duties but never to gather the fruits thereof. Let not the consequences of work be thy incentive, let there be in thee no tendency to inactivity. O Dhananjaya! Give up all attachments; perform your duties in pursuance of yoga. It does not matter whether you succeed or fail, but keep your mind unperturbed: the balance of mind and equanimity is called yoga" (11: 48) "He whose mind is unperturbed in the midst of sorrows, and is free from desires in the midst of joy, who is above passion, fear and anger, is a sage possessing stability of intelligence" (11: 56). "Such a perfect man does not desist from his duties, but his mind is free from attachment to the objects of senses. He achieves perfect peace and attains the Supreme Brahman" (11 : 64). "Greater is thine own work even if this be humble, than the work of another even if this be great. When a man does the work God gives him, no sin can touch this man. And a man should not abandon his work, even if he cannot achieve it in full perfection; because in all work there may be imperfection even as in all fire there is smoke." (18 : 47, 48)

4. Bhakti Yoga

The spontaneous love for the Divine is experienced by a bhakta. He is drawn to divinity by an irresistible, magnetic force of divine devotion. By his ardent love for God, he draws divine blessings to himself. The minute he thinks of Him, he is full of spirit and jumps with joy. He overcomes all obstacles, in fact he does not see them. He irresistibly calls the Lord, whole-heartedly attends to Him, and forgetting his own self is totally absorbed in Him. He most passionately and truly loves God. This is very rare. (Usually, what is seen is an emotional outburst of self-reverence. It could easily be mistaken for bhakti.) A bhakta may not understand or apply the science, techniques or methods of yoga for his self-development as would a jnana or a karma yogi, but he knows God. His life is automatically controlled.

Renunciation

There are those who lead a life of renunciation. Through their search for self-realization, they are able to overcome the desire for and attachments to material possessions.

For a Brahmachari (a would-be monk), a formal vow of celibacy, non-possession, non-violence, purity, chastity and modesty is appropriate.

Saucha

Cleanliness is next to Godliness. For mental and spiritual health it is necessary to purify body and mind. This is saucha.

Just as the state of the body affects our mood, our mind plays a vital role in the well-being of the body. Cleanliness does not only mean keeping the body clean on the outside. It also means getting rid of all impurities inside the body and mind. Just as the unclean outside is visually noticeable, the negative state of mind is revealed in the actions and behaviours of the bearer. Yoga teaches us to remove the inner impurities like anger, lust, jealousy, restlessnesses and impatience.

Yoga helps us to control our mind and senses in order to lead a healthy and wholesome life. Yoga philosophy says, we are a being of five sheaths (koshas) which interact with and are interdependent on each other.

The five koshas are discussed in detail in the chapter on Yoga Therapy.

Santosha

Santosha means contentment

A Santoshi is one who is not deluded into believing that this world and its experiences are real and final. He realizes that the physical existence is temporary. He remains unruffled in pleasure or pain, illness or health, praise or blame. He is in control of his mind and is able to act righteously in all circumstances. He carries out his duties diligently, sincerely, and with pure motives.

He does not waste energy to acquire material possessions and is content to satisfy his needs through honest means. A disciplined mind does not delve into useless speculations. The end product of work is seen as a culmination of an important on-going process through which one can experience joy and happiness. Belief in the karmic law of cause and effect ("what you sow so shall you reap"), enables one to accept the result of one's actions without pain or pleasure. Because one remains unruffled, maya cannot affect one.

A yogi is not ruled by greed or fear and is motivated by love. He has no expectations from others. He is able to maintain a calm, happy, fearless attitude to life at all times.

A santoshi has time to concentrate upon and to enjoy what he has and what he does. His freedom enables him to lead a happy and spiritually rich life.

This 'Niyama' leads to the practice of Ahimsa (no desire to hurt), Asteya (no desire to steal), Aparigraha (no desire to covet), and Satya (no desire to cheat or lie).

Tapa

The literal meaning of 'tapa' is to 'burn', 'to become hot'. In the context of yoga, the meaning is to develop self-discipline and to intensify spiritual zeal and yearning for God.

To don ochre robes and give up home and family life and to retreat to the Himalayas is not tapa. The *Bhagavad Gita* says: "false austerity for the sake of reputation, honour and reverence is impure. It belongs to Rajas and is unstable and uncertain" [Penguin version pages 112-113]. People who are peaceful and joyful in life, even when it is difficult to be so, have faith in themselves and in God.

A yogi methodically overcomes harmful emotions and thoughts to make spiritual progress.

The path of tapa is narrow and difficult. No matter how many times he falters, a tapasvi stands up bravely and strives again and again to perfect himself. He lives by the dictates of his conscience. His love for God makes him perform good deeds.

Tapa is the tool, swadhyaya is the radar, and satya (truth) is the core of reality. With the help of ashtanga yoga, a tapasvi aims to reach this core and that is reflected in his attitude, thought, words and behaviour. His life is peacefully active and actively peaceful.

Swadhyaya

Swa means self • Dhyaya means study

Swadhyaya (self-study) means the study of one's thoughts and emotions, so that we may wisely deal with them to make spiritual progress. A yogi carefully and calmly weeds out harmful and negative thoughts and cultivates positive and virtuous thoughts and actions.

A novice yogi, starting the practice of asana, pranayama and meditation, is certain to experience self questioning and answering. The process of dialogue with the self becomes more intense as one follows yama, niyama and other ashtangas in one's life.

It eventually accelerates the yogi's spiritual growth and frees him from the bondage of body consciousness.

Swadhyaya, like a radar, reveals to a yogi his thoughts, motives, emotions and attitudes. Yoga develops the positive aspects of these attributes.

Introspection becomes a swadhyayi's second nature. Every situation is carefully studied and analysed.

A Swadhyayi faces many conflicts – his conscience pulling him towards spirituality and the decent life, and ego pulling him towards worldly and materialistic life. A heroic disciple of truth patiently marches on. This war of Maha-bharatha (Spiritual War), constantly takes place in a spiritual aspirant. The conquest of ego ensures that the disciple will not be stuck at the Pratyahara (see Pratyahara) border incarnation after incarnation.

A sincere spiritual aspirant always wins in the end with the help of ashtanga, one's sat-guru, holy scriptures, and sincere prayers for right guidance and blessings.

Ishwara Pranidhana

means dedication of the fruits of one's work to God

Ishwara Pranidhana means to serve God with love and non-attachment wherever one is stationed in life. It means to render selfless service with faith and trust in Him.

The eternal master plan of the Creator passes through countless phases, evolving from one creation to another. Change is constantly taking place individually in each one of us, and at the same time collectively in the whole universe. We are constantly evolving through success and adversity, health and sickness, happiness and sorrow. These changes are to be viewed as different temporary patterns, neither better nor worse. They are to be learnt from, and not to be feared, or ignorantly adhered to.

A yogi always seeks truth. He executes his duties cheerfully and honestly. He works without being judgemental and accepts the results, whatever they are, favourable or unfavorable, good or bad. His every action is performed to the best of his ability not in the hope of one's personal gain or advantage, but as an offering of devotion to God.

आसन

Asana

"I stretch my body so that I may reach,
I teach my family so that I may learn,
I write my thoughts so that I may read,
I speak my mind so that I may listen."

The best known and most loved part of yoga is asana (physical exercise and posture), the third limb of ashtanga. Asana is a Sanskrit word and means a seat or a base. In any asana the body should be correctly postured and supported.

Asana is a science that helps us to know our body and mind better in order to develop our full potential. In practising asana, the body's energies are directed in a controlled but relaxed manner. In this way, the body's abilities and disabilities are realised. The body is held in posture correctly and comfortably to its full extent, but without straining. Adjustments must be made in one's movements and in the asana to work comfortably and to gain maximum benefit. The body should be allowed to move freely within one's limits. During the practice, questions will arise and answers will be sought from within oneself. This process of inner dialogue (swadhyaya), enables one to become aware of the relationship between body, mind and breath, and to use them for physical and spiritual benefit.

Benefits

In asana a yogi imagines various forms – that of a lion, a lotus, a tree, a locust, a cat etc. This helps him to understand, respect and love all 'Life'.

The innumerable benefits of asana include the limbering, strengthening, relaxing, controlling and calming of the body, mind and the breath. Generally all the body systems benefit directly or indirectly. At first, we may not notice all the effects which will be different in different individuals depending on the understanding and the effort. Some benefits, especially minor physical ones, may become apparent sooner. The metaphysical benefits are revealed through gradual and steady transformation of one's consciousness. Yoga becomes a way of life for a sincere, disciplined practitioner.

Asana lessens the body's toxic burden, by tackling waste removal systems. By contracting, expanding and relaxing the body, asana strengthens and flexes the joints, muscles and the nerve fibres. The lymph nodes squeeze and pressurise fatty tissues to release and drain toxic wastes from the skin, kidney, liver and other organs of the body. The energy previously inhibited by toxicity and inefficient functioning of the muscles, is released and channelled to improve blood circulation and functioning of the body and mind. Improvement is observed in one's ability to assimilate knowledge intelligently, to digest food; in the peristaltic movements of the intestines; and in the elimination and defecation processes. One feels refreshed and rejuvenated. The skeletal and muscular manipulations and adjustments in asana, besides freeing the joints and muscles of toxic waste as mentioned above, alleviate stiffness and pain. A healthy body keeps the body's heat normal, and nourishes the body's immune system. In asana practice the spine is correctly balanced and this enables the chakras (energy centres) along the spine to function properly. This results in beneficial pressure on hormonal glands and improved functioning of the entire endocrinal system. Good health, longevity, happiness and spiritual growth become part of normal life. Just as in Chinese medicine, stagnation or imbalance in the 'chi' is diagnosed through feeling the pulse and through the flow of the energy in the meridians, so in yoga the breath can reveal the state of one's body, mind and consciousness. Asana involves regulating one's breathing and this strengthens the lungs and other respiratory parts of the body.

It is important to recognise that incorrect/faulty exercises can deplete vitality and cause not only physical damage, but also restlessness, irritability and nervousness. If the symptoms of any ailments are unduly exaggerated or if your practice gives rise to a feeling of inexplicable pain, extreme heat, pressure, dizziness, fatigue or shakiness, then you ought to abandon the practice and relax. If you have doubts, it is best to seek advice immediately.

Asana Practice

A beginner should plan yoga lessons with some simple limbering and breathing exercises and easy asana. As the practice progresses, you may stay for a longer time in the simple postures already being practised. You may also include some intermediate postures. Later on, depending on your progress, your ability, knowledge and experience of yoga, you may add some advanced postures, pranayamas and bandhas and mudras.

Start yoga practice with a brief relaxation period. It helps to calm the body and mind. After this relaxation period do some simple movements to awaken and warm up the body and the breath. Initially, do not aim to stay in the postures for a long time, but just go through the movements with awareness of the body and breath. Adjust these movements according to the body's abilities and always work within your own limit. This way one's practice becomes more focused and dynamic, rather than aggressive. This holistically controlled togetherness of the body, breath and mind increases one's physical and mental abilities.

In the beginning, the amount of stretching, bending, twisting and particularly the holding of the body in a posture must be controlled in relation to one's capabilities. During the experiment, remain still and relaxed to obtain maximum benefit. Breathe normally when you first commence asana. Your aim is to learn to execute the postures as correctly as possible. If no specific breathing is required, the breath should be allowed to flow freely and should be observed in silence. It is most inadvisable to practise any specific breath control in the initial practice.

With the adjustments and alignments that continually take place at physical and mental levels in asana, the practice will become progressively easier, more precise, meaningful and enjoyable. If the above rules are followed each time, you will find that you are able to hold the posture with ease for a longer period. You will develop strength and establish harmony between the body, breath and mind. Deep rest, control and well-being will become part of life.

Initially, be patient and work within your limits. Do not allow your enthusiasm to get the better of your judgement and so strain your body unduly. Each posture should be executed and/or mastered slowly with confidence, care and understanding. As soon as any discomfort or distress is felt, discontinue the posture or make necessary adjustments. Always remember, Yoga, (Joy) cannot be experienced in discomfort and strain.

I must advise that short relaxation pauses should be taken between the practice of asanas. During these short rest periods, the energy awakened through the asana, spreads throughout the body and mind. Always finish the posture practice by relaxing in Shavasana (posture no. 1) or by meditating for a short period. You will enjoy the maximum benefits of an energised and relaxed body and mind, and the most fulfilling refreshing and healthy life.

Thirty minutes or so of proper yoga practice as explained is more beneficial, than an hour of hurried session. If you find it difficult to let go and relax, then you know for sure that you need yoga to help you develop a confident, relaxed attitude to life.

Always remember that everyone is unique, and that we all have different working abilities and limits. Never compare your practice or progress with someone else's; just do your best. Above all enjoy your sessions with an open mind and heart.

When you listen to your body, it will respond to you.

If you are pregnant or if you suffer from weaknesses and fatigue, have had recent operations or injuries, or if you are not sure, then it is best to discuss this with your yoga teacher. It is advisable to learn asana, particularly the strenuous ones, under supervision.

Just as a musician tunes his instrument, a singer tests his voice, or a dancer or athlete warms up his body before a performance, a yogi tunes his body, mind and soul before starting his day's activities.

The best time for yoga is in the morning, after attending to ablutions and bath but before breakfast. At other times allow at least three hours after a main meal and 1½ hours to 2 hours after a light meal. Food can be taken half an hour after the practice. Morning yoga is awakening and invigorating. It gives clarity of thought, confidence and control. Yoga, at the end of a hard and strenuous day, refreshes, revitalises and releases tensions and toxicity. Beginners may find it easier to practice yoga in the evening, since the body is more supple and mobile. In the morning, one may need to do more preparatory exercises before the asana.

A bright, warm, well ventilated room maximises the benefits. Weather permitting, it is beneficial to practise in the open air or with the doors and windows open. It is easier to relax in a quiet, airy place.

An exercise mat, a carpet or a rug is needed. A small cushion is useful in the sitting postures if you need to support the back. Wear loose, comfortable clothes that allow unrestricted movements and stretching. A tracksuit or a pair of shorts and a T-shirt are ideal.

Young or old, male or female, fit or not so fit, everyone can practise yoga, so long as each works within his or her own limits.

In illness or injury, take great care and even avoid strenuous and contra-indicated poses altogether. Seek guidance from a practising and understanding yoga teacher.

In order to develop fully, it is necessary to experience both group and individual sessions of yoga.

Yoga is for everyone

The Asana

The Asana

Adho Mukha Shvanasana or Parvatasana	66	Padmasana	105
Akarna Dhanurasana	101	Parighasana	53
Ardha Chakrasana	124	Parivritta Padma Janusirsasana	95
Ardha Chandrasana	50	Parivritta Paschimotanasana	100
Ardha Matsyendrasana	86	Parivritta Trikonasana	46
Ardha Padma Padahastasana	56	Parivritta Janusirsasana	93
Ashtanga Surya Namaskara	31	Parsva Konasana	78
Bakasana	119	Paschimotanasana	99
Balasana	96	Pasha Vakrasana	89
Bhujangasana	58	Patangasana	60
Bhujanga Padma Simhasana	112	Pavan Muktasana	74
Chandra Namaskara	135	Purna Matsyendrasana I	87
Chaturanga Dandasana	67	Purna Matsyendrasana II	88
Dandasana	79	Purna Utkatasana	38
Deepasana	115	Purvottanasana	72
Dhanurasana	64	Rajju Vakrasana	90
Dvipada Shalbhasana I	62	Sama Konasana	77
Dvipada Shalbhasana II	63	Sarpasana	59
Eka Pada Sarvangasana	126	Sarvangasana	125
Eka Pada Virabhadrasana	51	Setu Asana	68
Garudasana	42	Setu Sarvangasana	127
Gomukhasana	91	Shashankasana	97
Halasana	131	Shavasana	27
Janusirsasana	92	Siddhasana	106
Jathara Naukasana	61	Sirsasana	134
Koormasana	102	Sthambhasana	39
Kukkutasana I	114	Sukhasana	28
Kukkutasana II	120	Supta Janusirsasana	75
Lolasana	113	Supta Konasana	76
Malasana	103	Supta Vajrasana/Supta Virasana Series	82
Mandukasana	65	Tadasana	34
Marijariasana	73	Tara Mandala	29
Matsyasana I	69	Tolangulasana	107
Matstyasana II	70	Trikonasana	45
Matsyasana III	71	Upvishtha Vakrasana	85
Mayurasana	121	Urdhva Eka Padajanusirsasana	57
Moordha Padottanasana	49	Ushtrasana	84
Mrigasana	98	Utkatasana	36
Natarajasana	43	Utthita Tadasana	35
Naukasana I	116	Utthita Utkatasana	37
Naukasana II	117	Uttishita Moordha Lolasana	47
Padahastasana	54	Uttishta Pavan Muktasana	41
Padangusthasana	122	Vajrasana	80
Padma Janusirsasana	94	Vatayanasana	123
Padma Matsyasana	109	Virasana	81
Padma Parvatasana	106	Vishishthasana	118
Padma Sarvangasana	129	Vrikshasana	40
Padma Simhasana	111	Yogamudrasana	108

Shavasana

शवासन

Shavasana means corpse.

Shavasana deeply relaxes and energises the body and the mind.

Benefits

If properly practised, this powerful pose will tap into one's inner reservoir of healing energy. The total relaxation involved leaves one physically and mentally calm, revitalized and refreshed. Fatigue and extreme exhaustion are removed and nerves are soothed. Patients practising this asana daily whilst under medical treatment are guaranteed to recover faster. This asana is essential for people suffering from insomnia, anxiety, anger and physical or mental diseases, particularly those which are stress-related. The breath in the relaxed pose flows freely. It is an asana which rests and rejuvenates the body and mind immensely.

Through this asana one is able to learn to surrender and relax and attain freedom from negativity.

Shavasana is able to help in all circumstances no matter how trivial or complex the problem is.

Method

Lie flat on the back on a mat on the floor or on a hard bed and close the eyes. Keep the feet and the legs apart and loose. Keep the ankles, knees and hips rolled out. Keep the arms away from the body with the elbows slightly bent and the palms loosely turned up. Let the back spread wide and long and relax. Create more room in the hips and the shoulders by allowing them to spread. Relax the neck and the upper back. Rest the back of the head comfortably on the mat keeping it in line with the back of the neck and the rest of the spine. Let the lower jaw hang loose creating more room in the throat and mouth. Keep the tongue relaxed and swallow. Experience more room in the mouth and feel it moist and cool. Feel the face and forehead soft and smooth. The lips and eyes are kept lightly closed.

When the body is arranged like this and allowed to spread, an easy, comfortable feeling flows all over the body. You will automatically create and feel more room in the abdominal and chest cavities allowing all the organs there to adjust better, relax and energise. Remain aware of the harmoniously flowing breath and the comfortably resting body throughout. Relax for as long as you wish.

It is important that one practises Shavasana before and after a yoga session. The position can also be used between asana practice for short relaxation. This simple but extremely beneficial asana can be practised by anyone at any time.

Sukhasana

सुखासन

Sukha means happiness, comfort.

Benefits

This asana helps to maintain a comfortable upright posture. Physical and mental energies are engaged to support and nourish the body which functions harmoniously. It can be practised any time as it aids all activities. In fact, in India, this is the most commonly taken sitting posture. The crossing of the legs this way whilst eating allows the energy to travel up towards the abdomen and heart, aiding the digestive organs to function at their best and for the heart to generate positive emotions. This is why it is a common meal-time and prayer time posture in India. It is used for pranayamas, prayers, devotional services, meditation and relaxation. As its name suggests Sukhasana is to bring sukha (happiness) in one's life.

Method

1. Sit erect with the legs to the front. Fold the legs firmly in with the right shin crossing the left. Sit firmly and evenly on both buttocks and draw the folded legs close to the body. Straighten and arrange the back comfortably tall from the base of the spine to the base of the skull. Slightly pull the abdomen in and up and open out the chest by drawing the shoulders back and down. Bend the elbows, relax the arms and place the hands on the thighs with the palms turned up. Join the tip of the index finger and thumb in Jnana Mudra. Keep the chin parallel to the floor. The mouth, throat and tongue are kept moist and relaxed. The lips are lightly closed. Relax the face. Hold the head and neck upright in line with the back and lightly close the eyes. Maintain silence and stillness observing the breath as it comes. Observe and enjoy this comfort-inducing firmly upright, yet relaxed posture.

2. Open the eyes, unfold the legs and relax. Repeat by folding the legs the other way.

Tara Mandala

तारामंडल

Tara means star.
Mandala means shape or formation.

Benefits

A simple and yet most beneficial sequence, Tara Mandala is a powerful breathing exercise that strengthens lungs, chest, back, heart and arms and hands. For asthmatics it provides a corrective; strengthening as well as relaxing of the lungs. It gets all the lobes of the lungs working at their best. Tara Mandala vitalizes the body and mind and induces calmness. The ideal learnt through this sequence is to allow the heart and hands to work harmoniously together. Offer to all what you have in hand, and your heart will receive you home with joy.

Method

1. Stand in Tadasana (posture no. 5).
2. Join the palms in front of the heart 'in prayer position'. Exhaling, stretch the arms to the front at shoulder level, keeping the palms together. Separate the palms and turn them down and keep the arms shoulder-width apart with the fingers and thumbs together and stretched.
3. Inhaling, stretch the arms out to the sides. Make sure that the arms and palms are in line and at shoulder level. Keeping the fingers and thumbs together and pointed, exhaling, turn the palms up.
4. Inhaling, stretch the arms above the head. Keep the arms close to the ears, with the palms facing each other. Exhaling, twist the arms and palms out and lower the outstretched arms to the sides at shoulder level with the palms turned down.
5. Inhaling, turn the palms up and on exhalation bring the outstretched arms to the front with the arms shoulder-width apart and the palms facing up.
6. Inhaling, turn the arms in and join the palms together. Exhaling, draw the arms close to the body assuming the prayer position. This is one round of Tara Mandala. You may repeat this a few times if you wish with a short relaxation in the prayer posture in between sequences.

3

c

d

e

f

g

h

Uttishta Moordha Lolasana

Uttishta means standing.
Moordha means head.
Lola means swing.

उत्थिष्ट मूर्ध लोलासन

Benefits

Uttishta Moordha Lolasana strengthens the back, legs, arms, neck and hips. It improves the circulation of blood and energy all over the body and gives rest to the spine, head, heart and the nervous system. The digestive and elimination processes are aided by the practice of this asana. One feels physically and mentally refreshed. Calmness, well-being, confidence and clarity of thought are experienced.

Method

1. Stand with the legs approximately 3 ft. apart and the toes pointed to the front.
2. On inhalation, stretch the arms above the head, arch the back and neck and turn the face up. On exhalation, bend forward and down from the hips keeping the legs stretched and the feet firmly pressed. On exhalation, push the hips back and up, bend the elbows and grip the feet with the hands to lower the trunk further down. Bend the knees slightly and lower the trunk and the head still further. Take the arms back one at a time from in between the legs and entwine them round their respective legs. Place the palms on their respective feet. Gripping the legs firmly once more with the entwined arms, further raise the hips and lower the head between the legs. If you feel comfortable and confident, you may close your eyes. Breathe normally and remain aware of the posture and the breath. Relax as much as possible.
3. Untwine and release the arms one at a time and straighten the legs. Inhaling, raise the trunk and stretch the arms above the head to come up to the starting posture. On exhalation, lower the arms to the sides and bring the feet together. Relax.

c

d

Moordha Padottanasana

मूर्ध पदोत्तानासन

Moordha means head.
Pada means leg/foot.
Tana means stretch.

Benefits

The whole body is strongly exercised and toned in this asana particularly the hamstrings, calves, hips and the inner thighs. The blood flows easily from the hips and abdomen to the heart and from the heart to the shoulders, neck and head. The abdominal organs are toned and better adjusted, improving digestion. The posture strengthens and soothes the nerves and centres one's being. It stimulates memory and induces peace and a feeling of well-being. In this posture, the hands and feet are well grounded, to relax the heart. Likewise in life if one's hands and feet are used by choice to perform good deeds, one's heart is at peace.

Method

1. Stand with the legs 3 to 3.5 ft. apart with the toes pointing to the front and the hands on the hips.

2. Inhaling, bend the back and turn the head up to the ceiling. Whilst exhaling, bend forward and down from the hips. Keep the legs stretched, the feet flat and firm on the ground and push the hips back and up. Lower the arms and place the palms on the floor about 18 inches apart and 10 inches to the front with the elbows bent. Inhale deeply and while exhaling, press the palms in and push the tail up to bend the body further down. Lower and touch the crown of the head to the floor. In this posture there is no weight on the head. Breathing naturally, stay still and relaxed in the posture. Remain aware of the breath and the body.

3. Stretch the arms to the front and inhaling come up to the standing posture. Exhaling, lower the arms, bring the feet together and relax.

Ardha Chandrasana

अर्ध चन्द्रासन

Ardha means half.
Chandra means moon.

Benefits
Ardha Chandrasana strengthens the limbs, back, neck, chest, abdomen, shoulders and hips. One's digestion and elimination processes are improved. It makes one feel physically and mentally well. It develops will-power, concentration, patience and clarity of thought.

a

Method

1. Stand with the feet 3ft apart.
2. Turn the left foot out to the left and the right foot slightly in to the left. Bend the left knee and exhaling, bend the trunk to the left and put the left palm on the floor about a foot away in front of the left foot. Breathe in deeply, and on exhalation, press the left foot and the left palm in firmly onto the floor and raise the right leg up. At the same time, straighten and stretch the left arm and the left leg. Place the right palm on the right hip and stretch the right leg away in line with the body and point the toes. Adjust by balancing the weight firmly and evenly on the left hand and the left foot. Draw the right shoulder back and turn the head to look to the front. Remain as steady as possible in the posture for a few seconds without straining. Concentrate on the stable posture and naturally flowing breath.
3. On exhalation, gradually lower the right leg whilst bending the left knee and lifting the left palm off the floor. Inhaling, raise the body to the upright posture and straighten the left leg. Bring the feet together and relax. Repeat on the opposite side.

Note
As the posture is strenuous on the legs, it should only be practised after appropriate preparations.

b

Eka Pada Virabhadrasana

Eka means one.
Pada means leg/foot.
Vira means hero or warrior.
Bhadra is the name of a hero in Hindu Purana (ancient text).

एक पद विरभद्रासन

Benefits

This demanding posture forces the body and mind to work together and at their best. Blood circulation is improved in the entire body and all the systems are vitalized, strengthened and relaxed. Physical, mental and emotional strength and control are developed. The posture centres one's attention enough to create balance, poise and unity in the body and mind. In this posture, the superiority of the mind is seen clearly. Will-power, positive thinking, confidence, concentration, balance, co-ordination and precision are needed and are developed further in this superb posture. It helps align the left and right sides of the body and mind. It leaves one totally rejuvenated, refreshed and relaxed.

Method

1. Stand with the legs 3 to 4 ft. apart.
2. Inhaling, raise the arms out to the sides at shoulder-level. Stretch the arms and keep the fingers and thumbs together and stretched. Turn the left foot out to the left and the right foot slightly in to the left. Bend the left knee and exhaling, rotate the hips and the trunk to the left. Inhaling, raise the arms above the head, join the palms together and arch the back and the neck. Take the arms as far behind the ears as possible and fix the gaze on the hands. Bend the back as evenly as possible. Keep the right foot flat and firm on the floor and the right leg stretched. Breathe normally and comfortably and hold Virabhadrasana according to your ability.
3. Exhaling, bend forward from the hips and extend the trunk and arms to the front keeping the palms together and fingers pointed. At the same time straighten and stretch the left leg and raise and stretch the right leg and foot behind. Balancing the weight of the body on the left leg, whilst exhaling, further extend the trunk and arms to the front and the right leg behind. Both the legs are kept stretched all the time. Keep the hands, arms, trunk, right leg and right foot in a straight line. Fix the gaze on the hands or ahead. Hold firm the 'T' posture, i.e. Eka Pada Virbhadrasana and breathe as it comes.
4. Lower the right leg whilst bending the left knee. Raise the trunk and arms. Untwist the body, lower the arms and relax. Repeat on the opposite side.

a   *b*

20

c

d

e

f

Parighasana

परिघासन

Parigh means a fence, gate or border.

Benefits
The posture helps to keep the hips, knees, spine, arms and legs strong and supple, and tones the abdominal organs.

Method

1. Sit in Vajrasana (posture no. 47).
2. Kneel upright on the knees keeping both the feet relaxed. Balance the weight on the left knee and stretch the right leg out to the right in line with the body. Keep the right foot as flat as possible on the floor and the toes pointed to the front. Make sure that the right foot is in line with the left knee. Draw the shoulders slightly back and down. Place the right hand on the right thigh and exhaling, slide the right hand down the right leg and bend the trunk slowly to the right causing a stretch on the left side of the body. Make sure this is a sideward bend and not a forward/sideward bend. Place the right hand on the right foot. Inhaling, raise the left arm up and exhaling fully stretch it over the head and to the right keeping it in line with the body stretch. Keep the fingers together and stretched. Adjust by distributing the weight as evenly and firmly as possible on the left leg and the right leg and right foot. Adjust by drawing the shoulders back and creating an opening in the chest and shoulders. Turn the face to the upper left arm. Stay still for a comfortable period and relax as much as possible. Breathe normally and concentrate the mind on the posture and breath.
3. On inhalation, raise the left arm and the trunk up. Exhaling, lower the left arm, bend the right leg and sit again in Vajrasana (posture no. 47) with the palms turned up. Relax. Repeat on the opposite side to complete one round of Parighasana.

Padahastasana

पादहस्तासन

Pada means feet, legs.
Hasta means hands.

Benefits

An exceptionally beneficial asana which strengthens and tones the back, hips, arms, neck and legs and keeps the spine flexible. It strengthens the chest and abdomen. People suffering from constipation, dyspepsia and other gastric troubles benefit from practising it. By unblocking the energy meridians all over the body, tensions and stiffness are relieved. The brain is nourished through increased blood circulation. The hamstrings and para-spinal muscles are strengthened and relaxed. Padahastasana strengthens and soothes the nerves and stimulates memory, wisdom, intelligence and will-power. One feels rejuvenated, calm and refreshed after its practice.

The mind functions better when focused on where the feet are placed.

Method

1. Stand in Tadasana (posture no. 5) with the feet together.
2. On inhalation, stretch the arms over the head, arch the back and turn the face up. On exhaling, stretch forward and down from the hips. On the next exhalation, bend further forward and down and grip the ankles/toes with the hands. Stretch the legs, bend the elbows, and again exhaling stretch down a little more. Place the palms on either side of the feet or wedge them under the soles of the feet and put the head below the knees. Stay still in the deep forward bend for a few comfortable moments quietly focusing on the pose and the breath.
3. On inhalation, slowly raise the trunk to resume the standing posture and relax.

Note

This posture should always be taken on the out-breath, and should be practised with due care.

22

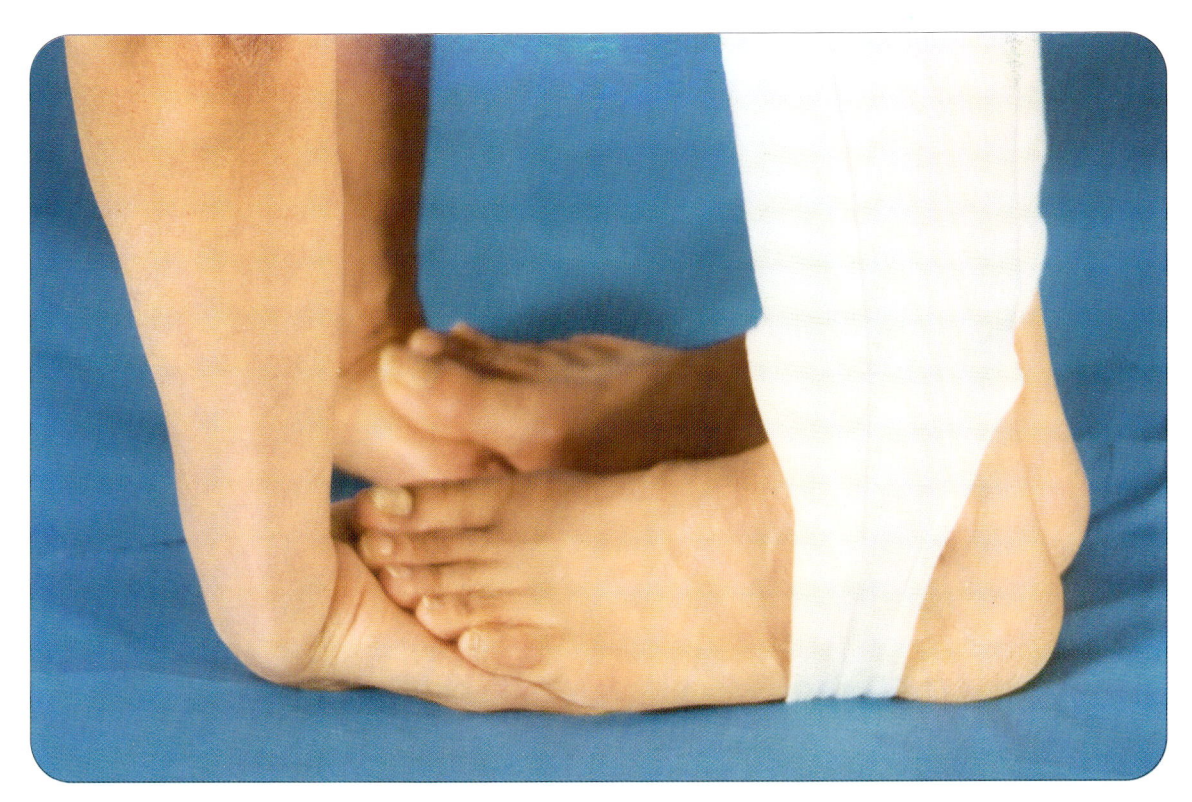

Ardha Padma Padahastasana

Ardha means half. Padma means lotus. Pada means feet. Hasta means hands.

अर्ध पद्म पादहस्तासन

Benefits

Strengthens and relaxes the back, abdomen, shoulders, legs, arms, chest and hips; in fact the whole body. It stimulates the abdominal organs and relaxes the heart, neck and head. This inverted asana increases the circulation particularly in the face, head and neck, maintaining a youthful appearance. It is a whole-body pose which helps tone all the systems. It strengthens and soothes the nerves, stimulates memory, concentration, will-power, intelligence and calmness. One feels vitalized, calm, comfortable, empowered and refreshed after its practice.

Method

1. Stand in Tadasana (posture no. 5).
2. Put all the weight firmly and evenly on the right leg and foot and flex the left knee. Raise the left leg and take hold of the left ankle and foot with both the hands. Twist the left leg out and place the left foot with the sole turned up, high up on the right thigh. Straighten the back and keep hold of the left foot with the right hand only and release the left hand. Twist the left arm, take it right round the back to the right hip, and grip the toes of the left foot with the left hand. On inhalation, stretch the right arm above the head, arch the back and neck and turn the face up. Draw the shoulders back and push the chest forward. Adjust and grip the left foot firmly. On the next exhalation, extend and bend the body forward and down from the hips. Keep the right foot firm and even on the floor all the time. On the next exhalation, further extend the trunk forward and down and push the hips up. Place the right palm flat on the floor beside the right foot. Lower the head as low as possible onto the right leg. On exhaling again, press the palm on to the floor, pull the abdomen in, push the hips up, and further lower the head. Breathe as it comes. Remain steady and relaxed in this inverted and knotted posture. Enjoy the mind strongly focused on the body. A well-earned refreshing and rejuvenating rest is experienced.
3. Stretch the right arm to the front and inhaling, stretch the body to the front and raise it. Take the right arm above the head. On exhalation, lower the right arm, and using the hands, lower the left leg. Relax before repeating on the opposite side.

Urdhva Eka Padajanusirsasana

**Urdhva means up. Eka means one.
Pada means leg/foot.
Janu means knee. Sir means head.**

ऊर्ध्व एक पदजानुशीर्षासन

Benefits

This asana immensely strengthens the back, pelvis and legs, particularly the hamstrings and calves. It particularly benefits sufferers with back problems, constipation, dyspepsia and other gastric troubles. The heart, neck and head relax in this pose. The venous blood rate is increased and the increase of oxygenated blood to the brain keeps the heart and face youthful. Will-power, wisdom and intelligence are developed and nerves are soothed and strengthened.

Method

1. Stand in Tadasana (posture no. 5).
2. On inhalation, stretch the arms above the head and arch the back and neck and turn the face up. On slow, steady exhalation bend forward and down from the hips. At the same time, stretch back the right leg and raise it as high as possible. Place the left palm on the floor beside the left foot and the right hand to where the right foot was. Balance the body's weight on the firmly and evenly pressed left foot and both palms. Stretch the right foot and point the toes. Bend the elbows and exhaling, extend the forward bend by stretching and lowering the trunk and head further down and to the left leg. At the same time raise and stretch the right leg and foot further up. Rest the forehead below the knee. Stay firm and steady and breathe as it comes. Focus on the strong and steady posture and the breath.
3. On exhalation, gradually, steadily and firmly lower the right leg. Inhaling, raise the trunk. Relax. Repeat on the opposite side.

Note

Extreme care should be taken when practising this advanced asana. It is best to learn this asana patiently to avoid unnecessary problems.

Bhujangasana

भुजंगासन

Bhujanga means cobra. Bhuja means arms.
Anga means parts of the body. A cobra uses his body as arms.

Benefits
This posture arches the spine from the top to the bottom. If practised properly, patiently and regularly, all the muscles, tendons, ligaments, joints and nerves in the spinal region are kept strong and supple. Bhujangasana stretches and tones the muscles of the abdomen and exercises the chest and arms, helping to relieve back pain, abdominal gas and flatulence. It helps to normalize the functions of the kidneys, bladder, liver and gall bladder. Constipation is relieved and menstrual problems are corrected. The asana also prevents hunching in the upper back. It strengthens and soothes the nerves, inducing calmness, peace and vitality. In this opening pose, confidence and security are developed as the cobra pushes forward its chest, heart and throat and holds its head high.

Method

1. Lie on the abdomen with the forehead on the floor, the palms with fingers stretched together near the shoulders and the legs stretched together and the toes pointed.

2. Turn the face up gradually to the front bringing the chin to the floor. Press the palms firmly onto the floor and whilst inhaling, raise the trunk off the floor by arching the back as evenly as possible. From the pubis downwards, the body should be on the floor. Take the shoulders back and down and push the chest forward and out. Keep the elbows slightly bent and the palms fully and evenly pressed down for better support. Look ahead or turn the face up. Firmly hold the posture for a short comfortable period breathing normally. Relax as much as possible. You may close the eyes or focus the gaze ahead. Focus the attention on the posture and the breath.

3. Keeping the head tilted back, on exhaling, lower the body slowly by bending the elbows further. Turn the face in until the chin touches the floor. Then slide the tip of the nose along the ground until the forehead touches the floor again. Bring the arms and the hands down beside the body. Turn the face to one side and relax.

Note
1) As long as the shoulders are not hunched, the arms can be stretched in this posture to extend the abdominal stretch and the arch in the back.
2) If one's back is not very strong and there is a problem holding in this posture, then either avoid holding or practise with the support of the elbows and forearms on the floor. Advanced Bhujangasana begins with the hands close to the hips rather than the shoulders. On inhaling, the palms are pressed, arms are stretched and the entire back is arched evenly from the pubis to the neck.

Sarpasana

सर्पासन

Sarpa means snake.

Benefits
Sarpasana strengthens the back, stomach, chest, arms, hands, shoulders and the neck muscles. It is an excellent breathing exercise. With correct and regular practice one can get relief from backaches, constipation, flatulence, belching, piles and fistula. The spine becomes strong and flexible. Sarpasana develops concentration, will-power and calmness.

Method

1. Relax on the stomach.
2. Place the chin on the floor and stretch the legs and feet, keeping them together. Interlock the hands on the buttocks with the palms facing the head. Observe the breathing. On a good inhalation, draw the shoulders back and raise the head, shoulders, chest and stomach off the floor. Hold the breath, stretch the arms and the interlocked hands back and raise the upper body further. Hold the posture and the breath for a comfortable period.
3. Exhaling, steadily lower the body to the floor. Relax with the arms besides the body, the face to the side and the legs apart. Rest until the breathing settles down to normal.

Patangasana

पतंगासन

Patanga means butterfly.

Benefits
This asana strengthens the back, hips, legs, arms, chest, abdomen and neck increasing circulation all over the body. As the lungs and the chest are strongly worked on, one's breathing ability improves. Minor digestive and breathing problems are alleviated. Those suffering from back pain or from bad posture could benefit from regular practice of this asana. Physical strength and suppleness are achieved. Concentration, calmness and will-power are developed.

Method

1. Lie on the abdomen with the legs stretched together and the toes pointed.
2. Place the chin on the floor and stretch the arms out at shoulder level with the palms flat on the floor. On inhaling, raise the head, trunk, arms and legs balancing the body on the abdomen. Hold the inhaled breath. Keep the legs, feet, arms and hands stretched. Close the eyes or gaze straight ahead. Hold the posture as firm and as still as possible for a short period consciously relaxing in it.
3. Exhaling, steadily lower the body to the ground and relax.

Jathara Naukasana

जठर नौकासन

Jathara means abdomen.
Nauka means boat.

Benefits
Naukasana strengthens the entire back, particularly the lumbar region. It allows the chest cavity to open and improves one's breathing capacity. It helps trim fat around the abdomen and improves appetite and digestion. A good posture for mental and physical strength and calmness.

Method

1. Lie flat on the abdomen.
2. Place the chin on the floor. Stretch the legs and keep them together. Stretch the arms and hands beside the body with the palms touching the thighs. On inhaling, raise the head, trunk, arms and legs together arching the back firmly and evenly balancing the body on the navel in a boat shape.

   The legs, feet, arms and palms are all fully stretched and raised with the trunk and head. Hold the inhaled breath and close the eyes or gaze ahead. Hold the posture steady for a few seconds without straining.

3. When ready to breathe out, lower the body gradually to the floor exhaling steadily. Relax and breathe normally.

Dvipada Shalbhasana I

Dvi means two.
Pada means legs/feet.
Shalbh means locust.

द्विपाद शालभासन १

Benefits

This asana strengthens the lower back, neck, shoulders, hips, pelvic floor and the abdominal muscles. It exerts beneficial pressure on the solar plexus and the lower nerve centres. It also aids digestion. It is an excellent exercise for the diaphragm, lungs, colon and gluteal muscles. It is also a good asana for those suffering from sciatic nerve pains, irregular menstruation, piles, flatulence, painful urination and diabetes. It strengthens the lungs, nerves and the will. Energy is guided to flow towards the navel centre and higher centres. Physical and mental strength are developed in Shalbhasana. One feels deeply relaxed and refreshed after its practice.

Method

1. Lie on the abdomen with the legs stretched together and the toes pointed. Keep the arms beside the body with the fists clenched.
2. Place the chin on the floor. Bend the elbows and put the fists beside the hips, with the back of the thumbs on the floor and pointing to the feet. Keeping the fists and hands pressed firmly onto the ground, contract the back of the thighs, buttocks and the lower back and inhaling, raise the legs, hips, lower abdomen and bent elbows off the floor arching the lower back in as much as possible without bending the knees. Close the eyes, hold the posture steady and the inhaled breath for a short and comfortable period of time focusing the attention on the body.
3. On exhalation, gradually and carefully lower the body to the ground. Turn the face to one side. Breathe and relax.

Note

Throughout the practice of this asana, the knees do not bend and the chin remains on the ground. Strength and flexibility are required and they are developed in the lower back by this pose. Beginners may start by raising one leg at a time.

Dvipada Shalbhasana II

द्विपाद शालभासन २

Benefits

For the Note and Benefits see Dvipada Shalbhasana - I (posture no. 29). The arms, shoulders, neck, back and hips work more intensely in this version.

Method

1. Roll on the right side of the body with the legs stretched together.
2. Stretch both the arms down in front of the body. Clench the fists with the back of the thumbs facing the front. Roll on to the abdomen with the arms as much under the body as possible, with the back of the thumbs and the chin on the floor. Press and push the arms and fists onto the floor, contract the back of the thighs, buttocks and lower back. Inhaling, raise the legs, hips and lower abdomen off the floor arching the back as much as possible without bending the knees. Close the eyes and hold the posture and the inhaled breath for a comfortable period of time.
3. On exhalation, lower the body gradually and carefully onto the arms. Draw the arms out, turn the face to one side and relax. Let the breathing rhythm settle down.

Dhanurasana

धनुरासन

Dhanu means bow.

Benefits

Dhanurasana exercises the deep muscles of the spine removing stiffness, aches and pains. It tones the chest, lungs and abdominal muscles and strengthens the ligaments and tendons in the spine, knees, elbows, hips, shoulders and neck. It works strongly on the spinal centres and nerves. It aids digestion and helps to relieve abdominal gas. It improves the functioning of the kidneys, bladder, genital, pelvic and other abdominal organs. An excellent posture for energizing and relaxing the whole body.

Method

1. Relax on the abdomen.
2. Place the chin on the floor and stretch the legs, keeping them together. Bend the knees and grip the ankles with the hands. On inhaling, raise the head and trunk arching the back evenly and deeply. At the same time, balancing firmly on the abdomen raise the thighs and push the feet up and away from the body to form a bow with the body. Turn the face up and hold the breath. Bring the back of the head and feet as close to each other as possible. Close the eyes or fix the gaze ahead and keep the attention focused on the pose. Keep the posture steady until the breath can be held comfortably.
3. On a controlled steady exhalation, whilst releasing the ankles, lower the body gradually to the ground. Relax on the side of the face. Let the breath flow naturally.

Mandukasana

मंडूकासन

Manduka means frog.

Benefits
Mandukasana strengthens and tones the back, legs, arms, feet, hands, chest and abdomen and all the joints. It helps correct hunched back and shoulders. Blood circulation and energy levels are increased. The posture helps develop physical and mental strength and calmness, and leaves one feeling refreshed.

Method

1. Lie on the abdomen with the legs stretched together, the arms close to the body and the chin on the floor.
2. Bend the knees and bring the heels onto the buttocks. Bend the arms and place the palms on top of their respective feet. Push the feet down with the hands and on inhaling raise the chest and the head. Hold the inhaled breath and the posture and keep the heels pressed to the buttocks and the knees to the floor for a few comfortable seconds. With the gaze either fixed ahead or the eyes closed, relax as much as possible in this simple-looking dynamic pose.
3. On exhalation, gradually lower the body and the arms. Straighten the legs and relax.

Adho Mukha Shvanasana (or Parvatasana)

अधो मुख शवानसन/पर्वतासन

Adho means downwards.
Mukha means face.
Shvana means dog.
Parvata means mountain.

Benefits

This asana helps to keep the back, shoulders, hips and other joints strong and flexible, and works strongly on the hamstrings, biceps and armpits. Lungs, chest and abdomen are toned. Head and heart are particularly relaxed in head-down postures.

Method

1. Relax on the abdomen with the side of the face to the floor.
2. Place the chin on the floor and the palms beside the shoulders. Stretch the legs and keep them together. Tuck the toes in, press the palms firmly onto the ground and raise the body on the hands and toes. Exhaling, swing and push the hips up and lower the head in between the arms by fully stretching the arms and legs. Lower the heels to the floor. Extend the back by raising the hips further up and by lowering and tucking the head deeper in between the arms. Adjust to balance the body firmly on the hands and feet. Close the eyes if you wish. Relax in the Shvanasana, breathing normally and remaining aware of the posture and breath.
3. On exhalation, bend the knees and elbows and lower the body to the floor. Relax.

Chaturanga Dandasana

Chatur means four.
Anga means part.
Danda means rod.

चतुरंग दंडासन

Benefits

All the four (chatur) limbs as well as the back, hips, abdomen and chest are strengthened in this simple-looking, dynamic pose. Chaturanga Dandasana improves breathing, digestion and blood circulation. It tones the whole body, improves concentration and relaxes the body and mind.

a

b

Method

1. Lie on the abdomen.
2. Put the chin on the floor and stretch the legs together. Bend the elbows and place the palms on the floor near the shoulders. Tuck the toes in and whilst exhaling, press the palms and toes firmly in and raise the whole body in a straight line balancing it on the toes and palms. Remain in the pose for a few seconds.
3. Gradually lower the body to the ground. Lower the arms besides the body, breathe in deeply and relax.

Setu Asana

सेतु आसन

Setu means bridge.

Benefits

This posture strengthens the entire back, abdomen, arms, chest and legs. It keeps the joints flexible and nerves healthy. The thyroid and parathyroid glands are stimulated. The blood supply to the neck, head, chest, abdomen and back is improved. As the navel region is at the highest point in this asana, the stagnant blood flows easily from the abdomen to the heart and lungs for purification. Setuasana deeply relaxes the mind. The solar point being the highest point, the body is drenched with the solar strength.

Method

1. Lie flat on the back with the legs slightly apart. Keep the arms close to the body with the palms flat on the floor.
2. Bend the legs and draw the feet close to the hips. Keep them hip-width apart. Press the feet and the palms onto the floor and on inhaling, raise and arch the hips and back off the floor to form a bridge between the feet and the shoulders. Close the eyes and relax in the posture observing the breath and the body.
3. Bend the elbows and bring them well under the bridge to support the back whilst placing the palms under the waist with the fingers and thumbs pointing out and the wrists turned in. Adjust and wedge the elbows on the floor, in line with the hands, by further pushing the hips and the lower back in and up and by tucking the shoulders under. Rest the weight of the body on the feet, shoulders, arms, hands, wrists and head. Take care not to cause undue pressure to the throat. Close the eyes and relax in the posture observing the breath and the body.
4. Keeping the back up, lower the arms beside the body. Exhaling, gradually lower the back to the floor, straighten the legs and relax.

Matsyasana I

मत्स्यासन १

Matsya means fish.

Benefits

Since the shoulders are drawn back and the chest is expanded, the breath becomes fuller in this pose. The circulation improves, especially in the throat, neck and head, and also in the shoulders, chest and lungs. Digestion is improved. The entire spine is toned. General posture is improved. Hunching is cured with longer and more regular practice of Matsyasana. Sinuses are cleared. It keeps the mind focused, alert and relaxed. Physical and mental strength and calmness are experienced after its practice.

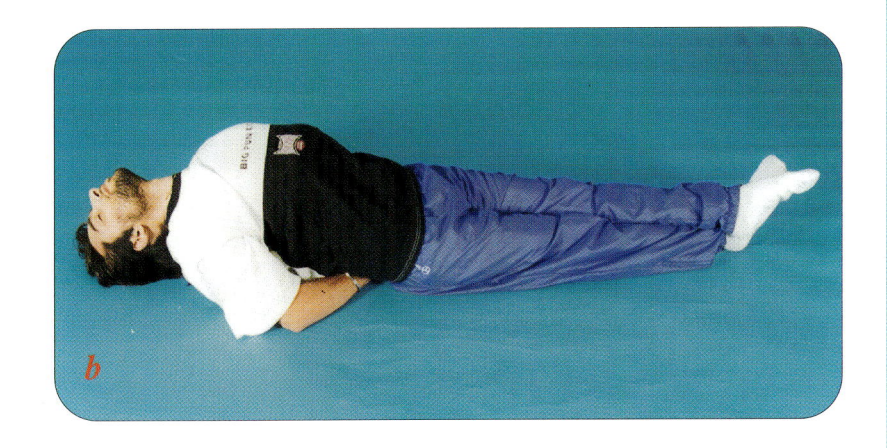

Method

1. Lie flat on the back with the legs together.
2. Bend the legs and bring the feet close to the hips. Raise the hips and place one hand on top of the other under the buttocks with the palms turned down. Stretch the legs and cross the ankles. Push the elbows and palms onto the ground and inhaling, raise the chest, shoulders, neck and head. Exhaling, arch the back and turn the head as far back as possible and rest the crown on the floor. Push up the chest and curve the back still further. Close the eyes and stay still in the posture without straining. Breathe normally. Focus the mind on the body and the breath.
3. Push the elbows and palms in and straighten the back and the head. Exhaling, lower them to the floor. Uncross the ankles, bend the legs and bring the hands out from under the buttocks. Relax the body. Repeat the posture crossing the ankles the other way.

Matsyasana II

मत्स्यासन २

Matsya means fish.

Benefits

This asana increases circulation in most parts of the body particularly in the back, neck, chest, throat and head. It regulates the activity of the thyroid. It tones the spine and stimulates the chakras (nerve centres) along the spine. The sexual glands, the intestinal and bladder muscles benefit from this exercise. People suffering from asthma and digestive problems would also benefit from its practice. Matsyasana strengthens and relaxes the body and mind. One feels alert, clear and calm.

a

b

Method

1. Lie flat on the back with the legs together and arms close to the body.

2. Push the elbows onto the ground by bending the arms. Grip the hips with the hands and while exhaling raise and arch the upper back and the neck. Turn the head as far back as possible and rest the crown on the floor. Bend in the legs and draw them closer to the body. Bring the soles of the feet together by widening the legs and lowering the knees to the floor as much as possible. Fold the arms on the chest. Adjust and be as comfortable as possible in this position. Close the eyes and hold the posture still focusing the attention on the breathing rhythm and the pose.

3. Unfold the arms, grip the hips and straighten the neck, head, back and legs. Relax.

Matsyasana III

मत्स्यासन ३

Matsya means fish.

Benefits
The back, hips, abdomen, neck, shoulders and limbs are strengthened in this asana. The chest cavity is expanded, improving the breathing. The functioning of the thyroid is improved. Common abdominal, back and chest complaints are relieved.

Method

1. Lie flat on the back with the legs stretched together. Keep the arms close to the body with the palms flat on the floor.

2. Bend and push the elbows into the ground, raise and arch the back and neck. Grip the hips with the hands and exhaling, turn the head as far back as possible and rest the crown on the floor. Stretch the arms close to the body and press the palms onto the floor. On inhalation, raise the stretched legs together about 30° to the floor. Close the eyes and stay still in the posture for a comfortable period and breathe normally. Concentrate on the pose and the breathing rhythm.

3. On exhalation, lower the legs to the ground. Bend and press the elbows onto the floor and grip the thighs with the hands. Straighten and relax the head, neck and the back. Relax.

Purvottanasana

पूर्वोत्तानासन

Purva means east or front of the body.
Tana means stretch.

Benefits

This posture strengthens and tones the arms, legs, back, neck, chest, abdomen, shoulders, elbows, wrists, hips, knees and ankles. It stretches and strengthens the front of the body just the same as the back and opens the energy channels. Digestive and elimination processes are improved. One feels fully stretched and light. Confidence, will-power and balance are developed. With the hands and feet forming the base and the body facing upwards in this asana, its practitioner feels strong, secure and confident.

Method

1. Sit upright with the legs straight to the front.
2. Place the palms flat about 12" behind the body and about 6" apart with the fingers pointing to the hips. Bend the legs slightly, press the palms and the heels firmly onto the ground. Inhaling, raise the body balancing on the hands and the heels. Straighten and stretch the arms and the legs fully. Lower the soles onto the floor as far as possible. Keep the body in as straight a line as possible. Adjust and balance strongly and firmly on the hands and feet. Stay in the posture and breathe normally. Remain aware of the posture and the breath. You may close the eyes or look straight up.
3. On exhalation, bend the elbows and the knees and lower the seat gradually to the floor. Bring the arms to the front and relax.

Marjari Asana

मार्जरि आसन

Marijari means cat. This asana is popularly known as Vaghrasana.

Benefits

Marjriasana is an excellent exercise for the spinal vertebrae, ligaments, tendons and muscles. The vertebrae become better adjusted by the extension, contraction and relaxation of the back in this gentle sequence. The wave-like movement of the back in line with the head and the hips on the firm and even base formed by the knees and the hands, develops a lot of strength and flexibility in the spine. This action is most beneficial for people with stiff backs and for beginners, as the back is exercised vertebrae by vertebrae. The posture is also good for the abdominal organs, arms, shoulders, hips, knees, neck and armpits. Digestion and elimination processes are improved as the abdomen is stretched, relaxed and contracted in the sequence. The smooth working of the spine strengthens and soothes the nerves and induces vitality, calmness and freshness.

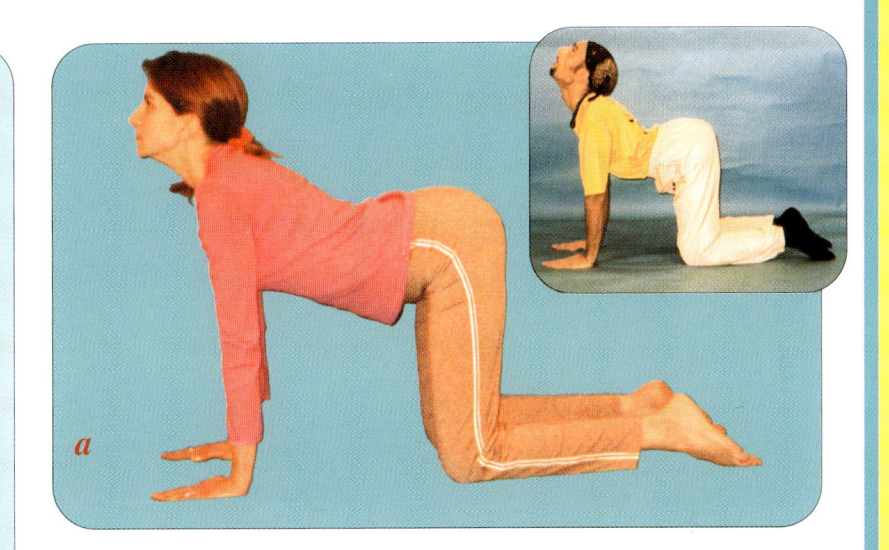

a

b

Method

1. Sit in Vajrasana (posture no. 47).
2. Bend forward from the hips, raise the seat and place the palms firmly flat on the floor about 15" in front of the knees and straight under the shoulders. Place the knees under the hips keeping them hip-width apart. The arms are kept stretched throughout the sequence. Lower the head between the shoulders and let it relax.
3. Press the palms and knees in to the floor. Inhaling, raise the head and the hips up and evenly curve the back downwards. Turn the face up, extend the neck and point the hips up. Adjust, and evenly distribute the weight on the hands and knees. Close the eyes and hold the posture without straining. Breathe normally and focus the mind on the balanced posture and the breathing rhythm.
4. On exhalation, the posture is reversed, i.e. lower and relax the head in between the shoulders and lower and tuck the hips in by arching the entire back and shoulders to form a dome-like shape with the back. Close the eyes and remain steady and still on all fours. Breathe as it comes.
5. On exhalation, sit back on the legs and lower the seat between the heels in Vajrasana (posture no. 47). Turn up and loosely relax the palms on the lap. Relax by bending forward from the hips on exhalation. Rest the forehead on the floor and the arms beside the body in Balasana (child pose). This is one sequence of Marjriasana.

Pavan Muktasana

पवनमुक्तासन

Pavan means wind/gas.
Mukta means release.

Method

1. Lie flat on the back with the legs stretched together.
2. Bend the legs and draw the feet near the hips. On exhalation, bring the bent legs onto the abdomen, loop the arms and hands over the bent legs and interlock the fingers. On the next exhalation, pull the knees and thighs down onto the abdomen, push the back onto the mat, and at the same time raise the head to the knees. Hold the position firm and steady for a few seconds.
3. On inhaling, lower the head to the floor and exhaling, release the arms and straighten the legs. Breathe in deeply and relax.

Note

If there is a lot of fat on the abdomen and in the buttocks area, practise this asana with one leg at a time.

Benefits

Pavan Muktasana helps to reduce fat on the abdomen and hips, thus keeping them firm and trim. It helps relieve accumulated toxic gas. It massages and tones the abdominal organs and improves the circulation and appetite. It creates a feeling of comfort and lightness. It increases mobility and strength in the joints and muscles of the spine, hip, leg and arm.

Supta Janusirsasana

Supta means supine.
Janu means knee.
Sir means head.

सुप्त जानुशीर्षासन

Benefits

The stretch in the back, legs, hips and neck is intensified (as compared to Janusirsasana – posture no. 58) in Supta Janusirsasana. This pose works strongly on the neck, abdomen, chest, back, legs, arms and keeps them in good working order. The hamstrings and abdominal muscles are strengthened tremendously. A calm and confident attitude is developed. Emotional strength, will-power and concentration are attained.

Method

1. Lie flat on the back with the legs stretched together, the heels pushed away and toes pointed up.

2. On inhalation, raise the left leg straight up until it is at a right angle to the trunk. Make sure the sole of the foot is facing the ceiling with the heel pushed up. Raise the arms and hold the back of the left leg with the hands. Keeping the back and the head on the floor, walk the hands gradually up the leg to the ankle/foot without bending the knee. Grip the ankle firmly by bending the elbows, and exhaling, raise the head and the trunk up to the knee using the abdominal muscles. Hold the position and on the next exhalation, bring the head as close to the knee as possible. Adjust and be comfortable in the posture. Close the eyes and stay as still and calm as possible for a few seconds. Allow the mind to settle on the posture and on the breath.

3. On exhalation, lower the back and the head and release the left leg. Lower the arms and exhaling steadily lower the leg to the floor. Relax the body. Allow the natural breathing rhythm to return. Repeat on the other side.

Supta Konasana

सुप्त कोणासन

Supta means supine.
Kona means angle.

Benefits
This asana stretches and tones the whole body relieving stiffness, aches and pains. It is good for strengthening the hamstrings and abductors. It is also an excellent posture for keeping the hips, neck, shoulder and ankle joints strong and supple. It relieves backache, tones the abdominal organs and trims fat around the hips, abdomen, upper arms and thighs. Stretching of this kind opens many energy channels leaving one vitalized and stress-free.

Method

1. Lie flat on the back with the legs stretched together.
2. On inhalation, stretch the arms out to the sides in line with the shoulders with the palms flat on the floor. Leave the right leg as it is. On exhaling, move the stretched left leg out to the left keeping it on the floor all the time as far up as possible so that the left arm and the left leg are parallel to each other. Push the left heel away from the body and point the toes to the left hand. Turn the head to the right. Adjust and be as comfortable as possible. Close the eyes and hold the posture firmly and comfortably. Remain still for a few seconds breathing as it comes.
3. On exhalation, move the left leg and both the arms down. Turn the face to the front and relax. Repeat on the opposite side.

Sama Konasana

सम कोणासन

Sama means even.
Kona means angle.

Benefits
Chest, arms and legs are strengthened. The spine, hips and shoulders are also kept strong and flexible. It is particularly beneficial for the lower back. It helps to relieve constipation, gas and belching. Excess fat around abdomen and hips is reduced. Physical and mental stress is relieved. It strengthens the nerves and develops will-power. One feels light, centred and full of vitality after its practice.

Method

1. Lie on the back with the legs stretched together.

2. On inhalation, stretch the arms over the head. Keep them close to the ears with the fingers and thumbs together and stretched on the floor. On the next inhalation, raise the stretched legs up together until they are at right angles to the trunk. Keep the soles of the feet flat to the ceiling with the heels pushed away from the body and the toes pointed. Hold the posture still for a few seconds and concentrate on the breath and the body.

3. On exhalation, lower the stretched legs steadily and gradually to the floor. On the next exhalation, lower the arms and relax. Let the body and the breath settle down. Relax.

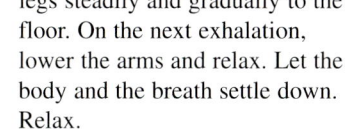

Note
People with a weak back should take extra care. They may have to begin by keeping the knees bent, or work with one leg at a time, or without stretching the arms over the head.

Parsva Konasana

पार्श्व कोणासन

Parsva means side of the body. Kona means angle.

Benefits

This asana exercises and tones the legs, pelvis, back, arms, shoulders and hips and strengthens the hamstrings and abductors. It is an excellent posture for keeping the spinal, hip, shoulder and elbow joints supple. It relieves backaches, tones the sides of the body and the abdominal organs and helps reduce fat around the hips, waist and abdomen. Stretching of this kind opens many energy channels leaving one vitalized and stress-free. It helps achieve physical and mental strength and balance. It alleviates nervousness, restlessness and other negativities. Concentration and confidence are developed.

Method

1. Lie on the right side of the body with the left leg resting on top of the right leg. Bend the left elbow and place the left palm flat on the floor in front of the chest. Raise the head, bend the right elbow and rest the head on the right hand making sure the right upper arm is in line with the body.

2. Bend the left leg in and bring the left knee close to the abdomen. Hold the big toe of the left foot with the left thumb, index and middle finger. Inhaling, stretch the left leg and the left arm up together balancing the weight on the right side of the body. In the beginning one might rock back and forth a little. In order to centre the weight, adjust the bent right arm, the stretched right leg and the body. Keep the right leg stretched and the toes pointed. Look straight ahead. Stay stretched and still in the posture for a few comfortable seconds breathing normally and focusing the attention on the posture and breath.

3. On exhalation, bend the left arm and the left leg together and bring them down. Release the toe. Roll on to the back and relax. Repeat the posture on the left side.

Dandasana

दंडासन

Danda means rod or staff.

Method

1. Sit firmly and evenly on the buttocks with the legs stretched together to the front and the back firm and erect. Push the heels away and point the toes up.

2. Press the palms with the fingers and thumbs stretched together and pointed to the feet, firmly and fully onto the floor beside the hips. Stretch the arms. Do not slouch or hunch the shoulders and make sure the shoulders and palms are in line. Keep the back evenly and firmly upright, slightly push the chest to the front and pull the abdomen in and up. Keep the chin parallel to the legs. Hold the head high and in line with the back. Relax the mouth and throat, look straight ahead and keep the gaze at eye level. Stay strong and still in the posture breathing normally for a comfortable period. Remain aware of the breath and relax as much as you can, whilst holding Dandasana firmly.

3. On an exhalation, release the hold and relax.

Benefits

An extremely good exercise for correcting a bad posture. This asana tones the entire body, especially legs, arms, chest, back, neck and abdomen. Since the trunk is upright and the seat firmly and evenly spread, the abdominal organs are adjusted and supported better. Digestion and elimination are improved. It opens the energy channels in most parts of the body, releasing physical and mental tension and other negativity. It helps develop concentration and will-power and gives physical and mental strength, calmness and unity. One feels refreshed, comfortable, calm and centred with its practice. This is one of yoga's most disciplining and grounding poses.

Vajrasana

वज्रासन

Vajra means solid, heavy, steadfast, rock-like determination and reliability.

This posture is used for prayers, pranayamas, relaxation and meditation. It is easier to keep the back upright in this pose than in many other sitting postures.

Benefits

This posture keeps the body's systems upright, exerting beneficial pressure on the internal organs, legs and feet. Vajrasana can be practised straight after a meal. The leg muscles and joints are exercised and vitalized, thus, keeping them strong and flexible. This supporting asana is particularly good for varicose veins, haemorrhoids and flat feet. Legs, when folded like this, ensure that the base of the spine is well supported and the back comfortably held upright. Thus, it automatically guides the eyes to turn up and focus at the eyebrow centre (Ajna). The asana relaxes the breath, nerves, and overactive brain centres - in fact all the systems of the body. It is an excellent pose for physical/mental stability, strength and calmness and it has an all-round grounding effect.

Method

1. Sit on the floor with the legs stretched in front.
2. Fold the right leg out to the right and bring it close to the right hip with the sole turned up. Raise the seat and sit on the right leg and heel with the upturned foot turned in. Similarly fold the left leg out and to the left hip with the sole turned up. Raise the seat and now sit firmly and evenly on both the legs and in between both the heels. All the toes should be spread on the floor with the big toes of both the feet touching each other. Make sure both the thighs and both the knees are close to each other. Turn the palms up and relax them loosely on the thighs. Alternatively, stretch the arms to the front with the back of the hands on the knees. Join the tip of the index finger and the tip of the thumb. Point the other fingers to the floor. This hold is called Jnana Mudra. Keep the spine erect, the shoulders drawn back and down and the abdomen gently pulled in. Keep the chin parallel to the floor, and the neck and the head in line with the back. Relax the mouth, tongue, throat and face. Relax and close the eyes or gaze softly ahead at eye level. Remain still and silent for a comfortable period of time, observing the breath and the body in this meditative pose.
3. Unfold the legs and relax.

Note

If at first the muscles and joints of the legs and feet are stiff, it may not be possible to practise this posture or to stay in it for a longer period of time. With perseverance and regular practice and by working within limits, the joints and muscles will get stronger and more supple.

Virasana

वीरासन

Vira means hero.

Benefits

Virasana strongly exercises the knees, hips and ankles, keeping them strong and flexible. It keeps the leg, back and abdominal muscles toned. The posture keeps the body's systems upright, exerting beneficial pressure on the pelvis, legs and feet and on the internal organs. It is a particularly good exercise for varicose veins and flat feet. Legs, when folded like this, ensure that the base of the spine is well supported and the back comfortably held upright. Thus, it automatically guides the eyes to turn up and focus at the eyebrow centre (Ajna). The asana relaxes the breath, nerves, and overactive brain centres - in fact all the systems of the body. It is an excellent pose for physical/mental stability, strength and calmness and it has an all-round grounding effect.

Method

1. Sit on the floor with the legs stretched to the front.
2. Fold the left leg out to the left and bring the foot near the left hip with the sole of the foot turned up. Make sure that the heel touches the hip. Likewise, fold the right leg out to the right and bring the foot near the right hip with the sole turned up. Sit in between the legs on the floor. Stretch the arms to the front and keep the back of the hands on the knees. Make sure that both the thighs and both the knees are as close to each other as possible. In order to meditate, you may join the tip of the index finger and the tip of the thumb of the respective hands and stretch together, as shown. Point the rest of the fingers to the floor. This hold is called Jnana Mudra. Sit firmly upright on the buttocks. Draw the shoulders back and down. Slightly pull the abdomen in and up. Keep the chin parallel to the floor. Relax the mouth, throat and face and keep the head and neck in line with the back. Keep the eyes focused ahead or close them. Remain in the posture for a comfortable period of time, observing the breath and the body. Focus the attention on the Ajna (between the eyebrows) at the forehead.
3. Relax the arms, unfold the legs and relax.

Supta Vajrasana and Supta Virasana Series

Supta means supine.
Vajra means unswerving, strong, firm.
Vira means hero, brave.

सुप्तवज्रासन / सुप्तवीरासन

Benefits

This asana tones the entire spine, working on all the nerve centres. The knees, hips, shoulders, neck and ankles are strengthened immensely. They, along with associated muscles are kept supple and pain-free. Circulation in the back, neck, chest, arms, abdomen, legs, throat, face and head is improved. One gets relief from the common complaints of the chest, back and the abdomen. The thymus and thyroid glands are stimulated. Bowel, uterus and bladder functions are improved. Diabetics could immensely benefit from its practice. The breath becomes fuller in this posture which makes it good for asthmatics. The nerves are strengthened and soothed. A combination of strength and flexibility in the spine keeps the body and mind strong and elastic.

Method

1. Sit in Vajrasana (posture no. 47) or Virasana (posture no. 48).

2. By reclining the back a little, place the palms flat on the floor behind the body about 6" away from the hips and 6" apart with the fingers pointing to the body. Bend the elbows and further lower the back down. Place the elbows one at a time on the floor. Hold the feet with the hands and exhaling, arch the back and take the head as far back as possible and place the crown on the floor. Adjust and arch the back evenly. The chin is now pointing to the ceiling. Close the eyes, relax and remain aware of the posture and breathe normally.

3. Grip the feet firmly, press the arms and elbows onto the floor, and inhaling, lift and straighten the neck and the upper back and rest them on the floor. Stretch the arms and hands close to the body. Close the eyes and observe the breath and the pose.

4. On inhalation, stretch the arms above the head. Keep them close to the ears. Stretch the hands and keep the palms turned up. Close the eyes, observe the breath and the body for a comfortable period.

5. Bend the elbows and join the palms together just above the head. Alternatively, fold the hands in front of the chest as in prayer. Remain silent and still in the posture and focus the attention on the breath and the body.

6. Grip the feet firmly again with the hands. Push the elbows onto the ground as before and raise the body to work your way back into Vajrasana or Virasana. Unfold the legs and relax.

Note
This is a strong sequence. It should be practised with care.

49

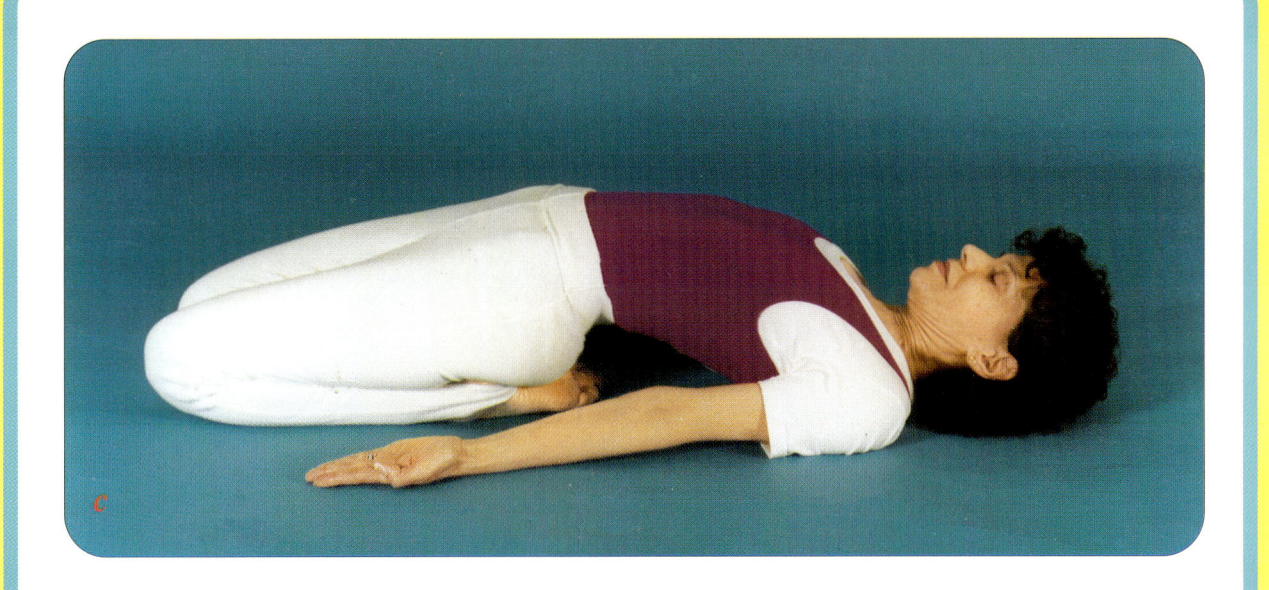

c

d

e

83

Ushtrasana

उष्ट्रासन

Ushtra means camel.

Benefits
This posture gives a deep curvature to the entire spine, thus increasing circulation in the deep and superficial muscles, toning the back thoroughly from top to tail and creating great flexibility. The neck, chest, abdomen and pelvis also get a good work-out in the pose, improving breathing, digestion, elimination and circulation. The asana helps alleviate constipation, piles, fistula, flatulence and back pains. It helps develop will-power, patience and mental and physical strength and calmness. It relaxes and refreshes.

Method

1. Sit in Vajrasana (posture no. 47).
2. Take the arms behind, twist them out, and grip the respective heels with the fingers inside and the thumbs outside the heels. Push down the hands firmly on the heels and whilst inhaling lift the body up on the knees and the lower legs. On exhalation, push the pelvis, abdomen and chest forward and up, taking the head back. Arch the entire back and the neck without bending the arms. Then place the right palm on the sole of the right foot and the left palm on the sole of the left foot and contract the buttocks and push forward the chest and collar-bone area. Adjust so as to even out the arch in the back. Hold the entire body firmly in this pose for a short period and relax as much as possible. Focus the mind on the pose and the breath. Closing the eyes is an option for those who feel comfortable, and wish to do so.
3. Grip the heels firmly once again with the hands and inhaling, carefully raise the head and straighten the trunk on the knees, and exhaling, gradually lower the seat to sit back in Vajrasana. Unfold the legs and relax.

Upvishtha Vakrasana

उपविष्ठ वक्रासन

Upvishtha means seated.
Vakra means twist.
This is one of the many variations of Vakrasana.

Benefits

If practised properly, this posture strongly exercises the entire body i.e. the front, back and sides, as well as the legs and arms, keeping the entire body strong and soft. It relieves lumbago pain and improves digestion, circulation and the general posture. The pelvic muscles are particularly strongly worked on. This simple looking pose demands attention and thus it develops concentration, will-power, steadiness and calmness.

Method

1. Sit erect with the legs stretched together to the front, the heels pushed away and the toes pointed up.

2. Inhaling, stretch the arms shoulder width apart straight to the front and at shoulder level so that they are parallel to the legs with the palms turned down. On the out-breath, gradually and all at the same time, twist the trunk from the hips, and the arms and face as far to the left as possible without leaning backwards. Moving from the hips will keep the buttocks firmly pushed onto the floor and both arms and hands in line. Holding the posture static is difficult in this deceptively easy-looking posture. Fix the gaze on the hands and breathe normally. Try and stay firmly upright, focused and relaxed for whatever period is possible.

3. On exhalation, gradually and steadily untwist, all the time keeping the seat firm on the floor and the legs stretched. Repeat on the opposite side. Relax.

Ardha Matsyendrasana

Ardha means half.

Matsyendra was a great sage, after whom this asana is named.

अर्ध मत्स्येन्द्रासन

Benefits
Lots of strength and flexibility are achieved as every part of the body is exercised. The asana particularly strengthens the back, shoulders, neck and the gluteal muscles. The working of the abdominal organs is improved. The twist in the back, abdomen, hips and pelvis helps relieve constipation, backache and lumbago. The twist in the abdomen, hips and waist helps reduce fat in these areas. It also helps to correct rounded shoulders. The body and mind are energised and refreshed.

Method

1. Sit firmly upright with the legs stretched together to the front and the toes pointed to the ceiling.

2. Keep the right leg as it is. Bend the left leg and take it over and to the outside of the right thigh. Place the left foot flat on the floor as near to the right hip as possible. Extend the left arm to the right and slightly twisting to the right, bring the back of the left shoulder as near to the inside of the left knee as possible. Bend the trunk forward a little, stretch the left arm and grip the right foot with the left hand. Twist the right arm out, take it as far round the back as possible and place the right hand on the left thigh. Exhaling, twist the trunk and the neck further to the right. Sit firm and adjust the trunk upright and rotate the trunk and head as far to the right as you comfortably can. Draw the right shoulder back. Close the eyes, relax the mouth and carry on breathing normally. Hold still for a comfortable period remaining aware of the breath and the pose.

3. After staying in the posture for a short period, let go of the right foot. In order to maximise the twist, slightly bending forward and to the right, twist and take the left arm round the left leg, and a little to the back by locking the left knee in the left arm. Push the right arm and hand as far as possible to the left and over the upper left thigh. Push the left hand up into the gap between the left shin and thigh and at the same time push the right hand down into the gap between the left side of the body and the left hip until both the hands clasp together. Lock the left leg firmly in and make the twist stronger. Adjust, sit tall and firm and avoid leaning back or forward. Close the eyes, relax the mouth and hold the posture for a comfortable period, remaining conscious of the breath and posture.

4. Release the hands. Untwist the arms and the body. Uncross the legs and relax. Repeat on the opposite side.

Purna Matsyendrasana I

Purna means full.

Matsyendra was a sage, after whom this asana is named.

पूर्ण मत्स्येन्द्रासन १

Benefits

Lots of strength and flexibility are achieved as every part of the body is exercised. The asana particularly strengthens the back, shoulders, neck and the gluteal muscles. The working of the abdominal organs is improved. The twist in the back, abdomen, hips and pelvis helps relieve constipation, backache and lumbago. The twist in the abdomen, hips and waist helps reduce fat in these areas. It also helps to correct rounded shoulders. The body and mind are energised and refreshed.

Method

1. Sit on the floor with the legs stretched together to the front and the toes pointed up.

2. Bend the left leg and take it over and to the outside of the right thigh. Place the left foot flat on the floor as near to the hip as possible. Fold the right leg in so the right foot is near the left hip. Extend the left arm to the right bringing the left shoulder to the inside of the left knee. Twisting the body to the right, loop and wrap the left arm around the left knee and take it as far to the left and back as possible. By adjusting the left shoulder and twisting the left arm further to the left and back, pull the left knee close to the abdomen and chest with the looped arm. Twist and take the right arm round the back and as far to the left as possible. Sitting firmly, whilst exhaling, turn and twist the upper body and neck to the left. Clasp both hands firmly at the back and towards the left side. Sit as firmly upright as possible and twist further to the left. Draw the shoulders back, clasp the hands firmly and open out the collar-bone area. Gaze ahead or close the eyes, focus and hold for a short and comfortable period of time.

3. Unclasp the hands, untwist and relax. Repeat when ready on the opposite side.

Purna Matsyendrasana II

Purna means full.

Matsyendra was a sage. This asana is named after him.

पूर्ण मत्स्येन्द्रासन २

Benefits
Benefits are the same as those in Ardha Matsyendrasana but the effect is intensified in this posture.

Method

1. Sit on the floor with the legs stretched together to the front and the toes pointed up.
2. Bend the left leg and take it over and to the outside of the right thigh. Place the left foot flat on the floor as near to the right hip as possible. Fold the right leg in and bring the right foot near the left buttock. Put the left hand on the sole of the right foot and the right hand on top of the left foot. Exhaling, steadily turn and twist the trunk with the head to the left. Extend the right arm to the left and bring the right shoulder round the outside of the left knee. Bend forward a little and twist to the left. Twist the whole of the right arm out and take it round the left leg and the back. Adjust by pulling the left knee in, close to the abdomen and chest. This allows the chest to open, and extend the right arm to intensify the twist. Twist the left arm and take it as far round the back as possible and clasp the hands. On exhalation, twist the trunk further to the left, and turn the head to the right. Sit straight, tall and firm in the posture. Close the eyes or fix the gaze ahead and concentrate on the breath and the twist. Remain in the posture for a comfortable period of time, relaxing as much as possible.
3. Release both the hands, untwist the body and straighten the legs and relax. After a short rest repeat on the opposite side.

Pasha Vakrasana

पाश वक्रासन

**Pasha means a cord.
Vakra means twisted.**

Benefits
A good posture for the back, ankles, knees and hip joints. The nerves are toned and the abdominal organs are strengthened, aiding digestion and elimination. Twists, bends and knots occur in life to strengthen us.

Method

1. Sit with the legs to the front.
2. Bend the right leg in and bring the sole of the right foot inside the left thigh and near to the groin. Fold the left leg out to the side bringing the left foot near the left hip. Twist a little to the left and lift the left foot and leg with the left hand. Raise the left leg, and rotating out the left hip and the left thigh, balance the left leg on the left knee. Rest the left ankle/foot on the left forearm and elbow. Interlock the fingers around the left leg and foot. Straighten the back and sit tall. Draw the shoulders back, turn the head to the right and fix the gaze ahead or close the eyes. Breathing normally, stay still in the posture for a short period. Focus the attention on the posture and on the breath.
3. Release the fingers. Holding the left ankle with the hands, lower the left leg down to the floor. Straighten the legs and relax. Repeat on the other side.

Rajju Vakrasana

रज्जु वक्रासन

Rajju is a rope.
Vakra means twisted.

Benefits

Most of the joints and muscles are worked on intensely in this posture, giving them strength, flexibility and lightness. The abdominal organs are rigorously exercised, aiding digestion, assimilation and elimination. The muscles and joints of the limbs and back are particularly toned. Hip and abdominal fat is trimmed. The nerves are nourished giving mental as well as physical strength and calmness. Its practice improves concentration, endurance and physical/mental co-ordination.

Method

1. Squat on the floor with the feet flat and together. Keep the knees together.

2. Press the semi-clenched right fist onto the floor near the right hip and on exhalation twist the trunk to the right. Bend the left arm and bring the back of the left shoulder over to the outside of the right knee. On exhalation, bend forward and twist the body to the right a little and twist out and take the left arm round the knees to the left and back until the hand is as near to the left hip as possible. Adjust and sit as upright as possible. Twist out and take the right arm round the back. Adjust the body and clasp the hands near the left hip. Rotate the trunk and the neck as far to the right as possible by clasping the hands firmly, and by pulling the legs further in. Keep the rotated trunk as upright as possible. Fix the eyes ahead, or if comfortable, close them and hold the posture still and breathe as it comes.

3. Release the hands, untwist and relax. Repeat on the opposite side after a short rest.

Gomukhasana

गोमुखासन

Go means cow.
Mukha means face/head.

Benefits
Like all the postures, this posture improves circulation, increases energy and relieves stiffness. It particularly works on shoulders, chest, arms, abdomen, hips, legs and back. It is an extremely beneficial posture for those with asthma or back trouble. It improves the functioning of the lungs and abdomen. It is a good grounding and at the same time an uplifting pose. Interiorization and concentration of the mind takes place easily and naturally with the practice of this asana. It removes feelings of weakness and fatigue and leaves one feeling well, calm and refreshed.

Method

1. Sit with the legs stretched to the front.
2. Fold the right leg in under the left leg, bring the right foot facing up, near the left hip. Fold the left leg in over the right leg bringing the left foot facing up near the right hip. This way the left knee is resting on the right knee and both the feet are facing up besides the opposite hips. Make sure not to sit on the heels or the feet. Sit erect and firm on both buttocks. Keep the legs firmly folded in and yet relaxed. Bend the left arm, raise the left elbow up in line with the left ear and take the left hand down the back. Twist the right arm out, take it round the back, bend the elbow and slide the arm as high up the back as possible. Adjust, by opening the chest out and forward and by drawing the shoulders back, clasp the hands firmly behind. Sit tall and firm on both the buttocks. Keep the chin parallel to the ground, close the eyes or look straight ahead. Relax and focus the attention on the posture and the breathing pattern.
3. Release the hands, lower the arms, uncross the legs and relax. Repeat on the opposite side by folding the left leg in first under the right leg, and by raising the right elbow up to the right ear.

Janusirsasana

जानुशीर्षासन

Janu means knee.
Sir means head.

Benefits
A maximum stretch in the back and the legs is obtained in this posture. It improves the circulation and energy level. This asana tones the back, the chest and abdominal organs. It gives physical and mental strength and rest. It leaves one feeling well, strong, calm and collected. All the chakras, from Muladhara to Ajna are strongly worked on.

Method

1. Sit firmly upright with the legs stretched straight to the front.

2. Fold the left leg in, place the sole of the left foot against the inside of the upper right thigh with the left knee on the floor as far to the left as possible. Keep the right leg stretched, the heel of the foot pushed away and the toes pointed up. Sit tall and firm on the buttocks. On exhaling, slowly bend forward from the hips. Pause at the end of exhalation. Breathe in and again exhaling, extend the trunk further down over the leg, grip the right ankle with both hands. Hold a while, inhale and on exhaling, again extend the stretch in the back to its maximum and clasp the right foot/toes with the hands. Bend the elbows, rest the forehead on the leg below the knee and lower the abdomen and chest as close to the leg as possible. Keep the back as flat and straight as possible. Close the eyes and remain still in the posture. Focus deeply on the stretch and the breath and relax as much as possible.

3. Release the foot and on inhaling, slowly raise the trunk. Straighten the left leg and relax. Enjoy vitality and calmness. After relaxation repeat on the other side.

Parivritta Janusirsasana

Parivritta means rotated.
Janu means knee.
Sir means head.

परिवृत जानुशीर्षासन

Benefits
A strong twist and extension in the entire trunk and neck is achieved in this posture. The back, pelvis, legs, abdomen, armpits, arms, chest and shoulders are well exercised. The whole body is toned and relaxed. All the systems of the body are aided to work happily and harmoniously. The asana particularly vitalizes the chest and abdominal organs helping to alleviate breathing and digestive problems and sinus and chest congestions.

Method

1. Sit upright with the legs stretched together to the front.
2. Bend the left leg in and place the sole of the left foot against the inside of the upper right thigh and the knee on the floor as far to the left as possible. Keep the right leg stretched, the heel of the foot pushed away and the toes pointed up. Sit tall and firm. On exhalation slightly bend forward from the hips. Twist and turn the trunk and the neck to the left and stretch the right arm forward. Twist the extended right arm out so that the right palm is facing the instep of the right foot. Grip the right instep with the right hand. Pause for a second, and whilst exhaling twist the trunk and neck further to the left, and stretch and bend the body forward as far over the right leg as possible by bending the right elbow. Inhaling, raise the left arm up steadily and exhaling take it over the head. At the same time maximise the twist and the forward stretch. Grip the outside of the right foot with the left hand. Turn the head up and fix the gaze on the upper left arm or close the eyes. Stay firm and steady in the posture and experience the stretch and the twist. Relax and breathe easily.
3. Release the right foot, and inhaling, raise the trunk, straighten the left leg and relax. Repeat on the other side.

Padma Janusirsasana

Padma means lotus.
Janu means knee.
Sir means head.

पद्म जानुशीर्षासन

Benefits
A maximum stretch in the back and the legs is achieved in this posture. The nerve centres along the back are stimulated and the energy meridians are opened, freeing blockages and tensions. The whole body is exercised and massaged, particularly the legs, pelvis, armpits, arms, abdomen, chest, back, shoulders and ankles. One feels physically and mentally calm and vitalized after its practice.

Method

1. Sit upright with the legs stretched to the front.
2. Bend the left leg in and with both hands put the left foot, with the sole turned up high on the right thigh. Stretch the right leg, push the right heel away from the body and keep the toes pointed up. Twist out and take the left arm round the back and grip the toes of the left foot with the left hand. Sitting firmly on the buttocks, stretch the right arm to the right foot, and exhaling, bend forward from the hips. Grip the right foot with the right hand, bend the elbow, and again exhaling, extend the trunk further forward. Adjust the left arm and grip the left foot firmly and comfortably. On exhalation, once more extend and stretch forward. Put the forehead near the right knee. Close the eyes and stay still in the posture. Breathe normally and focus the mind on the firm, strong stretch and the breath.
3. Release the right foot, raise the trunk, release the left foot, unfold the left leg with the hands and relax. Repeat on the opposite side.

Parivritta Padma Janusirsasana

Parivritta means twisted.
Padma means lotus.
Janu means knee.
Sir means head.

परिवृत पद्म जानुशीर्षासन

Benefits

This posture gives a strong work out to the body and mind improving the functioning of all the organs. The muscles and joints are toned and flexed, particularly the back, legs, pelvis, arms, chest and shoulders. Backaches and constipation are relieved and the digestion improved. It tones and firms the abdomen, hips and waist. The practitioner learns to breathe and survive in difficult knotted circumstances. The asana leaves one feeling well, calm, rejuvenated and refreshed.

Method

1. Sit firmly upright with the legs stretched together to the front.

2. Bend the left leg in, and with both hands place the foot with the sole turned up high on the right thigh. Push the heel of the right foot away from the body, and point the toes up. Sit firm and tall and on exhaling, bend forward from the hips. Twist the right arm out and hold the instep of the right foot with the right hand. On the next exhalation, further bend forward and at the same time, rotate the trunk to the left. On inhalation, raise and stretch the left arm up, exhaling, stretch it right over the head and grip the outside of the right foot with the left hand. Adjust to sit firm and comfortable. On the next exhalation, bend, rotate and stretch further if you can. Turn the head to the left and fix the gaze on the upper left arm or close the eyes. Stay firm and quiet in the posture. Breathe naturally and focus the attention on the body and the breath.

3. Release the right foot, inhaling raise the trunk, straighten the left leg and relax. Repeat on the other side.

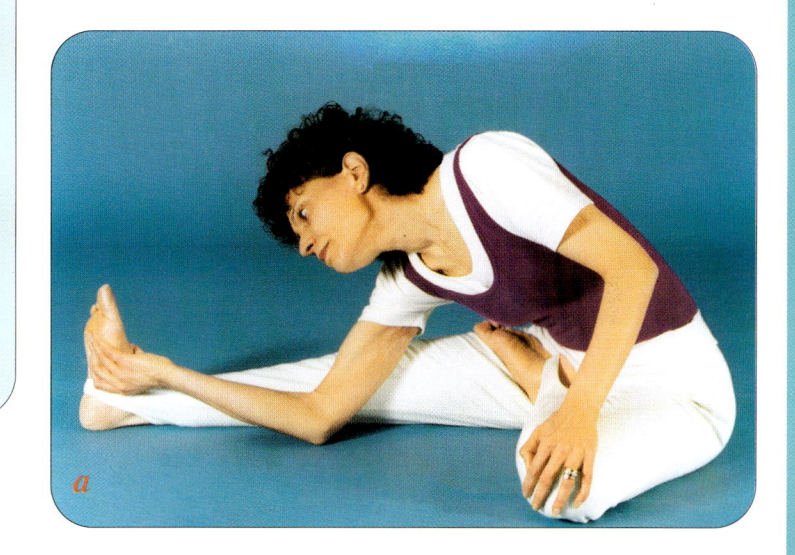

Balasana

बालासन

Bala means child.

Benefits

The child pose is primarily a relaxation pose. It is commonly used after the backward bending postures to relax the body and soothe the nerves. One's physical, mental and emotional being is comforted and made to feel secure in this spontaneous, natural and child-like position. It relaxes the mind and heart and calms the breath and the pulse rate.

Method

1. Sit in Vajrasana (posture no. 47).
2. Keeping the buttocks firm between the heels, on exhalation, bend forward from the hips. Rest the forehead on the floor in front of the knees and relax the arms beside the body with the elbows bent and the palms loosely turned up. Close the eyes, and breathing normally, remain relaxed in the posture. On inhalation, raise the trunk. Unfold the legs and relax.

Shashankasana

शशांकासन

Shashanka means rabbit.

Benefits
An excellent posture for giving a good stretch to the posterior muscles of the back and the neck. The abdomen and lungs are toned, the breathing and circulation are improved and the thyroid glands are stimulated in Shashankhasana. With the spine stretched, the head grounded, and the feet and hands together, the harmony flows in one's thought, speech and actions. Shashankhasana stimulates memory, wisdom, will-power and intelligence giving lightness, refreshment and energy.

Method

1. Sit in Vajrasana (posture no. 47).
2. Take the arms behind the body and firmly grip the feet from the outside with the hands. Raise the seat and, exhaling, extend and bend the trunk forward from the hips, arching out and stretching the back and the neck. Place the crown of the head on the floor in front of the knees. Do not put any weight on top of the crown or lock the chin to the chest. Hold the exhaled breath and this strong back opening posture steady, without straining.
3. Turn the face to the front and, inhaling, raise the head and the body and resume Vajrasana. Unfold the legs and relax.

Mrigasana

मृगासन

Mrig means deer.

Benefits
Mrigasana stretches and tones the entire back. It works on the abdomen, hips, chest, lungs, arms, legs and hands. Intense working in the shoulders, elbows, neck and wrists strengthens the tendons and ligaments and keeps them mobile. Deeper, fuller breathing is experienced immediately after the pose. Memory and intelligence are sharpened. Calmness, will-power and wisdom are developed.

Method

1. Sit in Vajrasana (posture no. 47).
2. Take both arms behind and join the palms together with the fingers pointing down. Exhaling, bend forward from the hips keeping the buttocks on the heels. Stretch the back and the neck and place the top of the head on the floor in front of the knees. On inhaling, raise the arms up behind and, exhaling, turn the enjoined hands down to point the fingers to the back. Close the eyes, hold the posture and relax as much as possible.
3. Turn the hands to point the fingers up. Close the eyes, hold the posture and relax as much as possible.
4. Slowly turn the face to the front by briefly brushing the forehead, nose and chin across the ground and, deeply inhaling, raise the head and the trunk to resume the initial Vajrasana posture (posture no. 47). Unfold the legs and relax.

Paschimotanasana

पश्चिमोत्तानासन

Paschima means west – back of the body. Tana means pull/stretch.

Benefits

This asana gives a full-length stretch to the back and the legs, keeping the spine strong and flexible. Circulation is improved, particularly in the chest, abdomen, legs, back and pelvic region. Nerves are toned and soothed. One feels physically and mentally rejuvenated and relaxed. Just as we try to relax and not strain when we stretch the back and the legs at the same time in this asana, we are taught to relax and understand the difficult and trying situations in order to progress. Patience, strength and humility are thus developed.

a

b

Method

1. Sit firm and erect with legs stretched together to the front. Point the toes up and push the heels away. Keep the trunk at right angles to the legs.

2. On exhalation, start bending forward from the hips. Hold the legs with the hands, bend the elbows and extend the forward stretch so as to bring the back as flat and as parallel to the legs as possible. Do this slowly, taking care to stretch fully (not only the upper back, shoulders and arms), to enable a fully balanced extension of the back and the proper working from the hips. Take a deep breath and on exhalation, keeping the elbows still bent, pull the trunk further forward by gripping the toes or feet with hands. When you have stretched to your maximum, take the hands around the feet, and rest the head below the knees. Keep the body as parallel to the legs as possible. Adjust to sit firmly on both buttocks and to keep the legs stretched on the floor all the time. Close the eyes, relax as much as you can in the pose and quietly observe the breath and the body.

3. On exhalation, stretch the arms, hands and back further forward and place the palms flat on the floor beside the feet. Stay in the posture without straining. Keep the mind on the posture and the natural breathing rhythm.

4. On inhalation, raise the trunk and relax.

Parivritta Paschimotanasana

Parivritta means rotated.
Paschim means west – back of the body.
Tana means pull/stretch.

परिवृत पश्चिमोत्तानासन

Benefits

This asana gives a full-length stretch to the back and legs. The twist works the spinal muscles strongly and deeply. The blood circulation is increased all over the body, particularly in the neck, back, chest, arms, legs and abdomen. This powerful abdominal exercise stimulates the liver, kidneys and pancreas, and helps to improve digestion and elimination. Most of the joints and muscles are worked on. Breathing is improved as the chest, abdomen and the back are forced to work in this difficult stretching and twisting pose. This asana brings strength and stillness to the mind. It tones and soothes the nerves leaving one energised, relaxed, refreshed and peaceful.

Method

1. Sit firm and erect with the legs stretched together to the front, with the toes pointed up and the heels pushed away. Keep the trunk at right angles to the legs.

2. On exhalation, bend forward from the hips, extend the arms to the front and cross the left arm over the right arm. Twist the arms out and grip the left foot with the right hand and the right foot with the left hand. On the next exhalation, bend forward further, bend and spread the elbows, rotate the trunk and the neck to the left, and lower the head between the arms. Adjust to sit firm and to further extend the back and to twist the body and neck as far to the left as possible. Turn the face up to look at the upper left arm. Fix the gaze on the upper left arm or close the eyes. Breathe naturally and stay as firm, relaxed and as quiet as possible in the posture for a few comfortable seconds. Focus the mind on the posture and breath.

3. Release the feet, untwist and inhaling, raise the trunk. Relax. Repeat by crossing the right arm over the left arm and twisting to the right.

Akarna Dhanurasana

A means towards.
Karna means ear.
Dhanu means bow.

आकर्ण धनुरासन

Benefits

All the joints and muscles of the legs and arms are exercised and kept strong and supple. The chest, neck, back, hips and abdominal muscles are strengthened. The posture tones the whole body. There is an increase in the ability of the body and mind to cope and to endure. Energy channels are unblocked, easing the flow of energy. One feels physically and mentally vitalized and relaxed.

Method

1. Sit firm and upright with the legs stretched together to the front and the heels pushed away.

2. Bend forward from the hips and grip the big toes of the feet with the thumb, index and middle fingers of the respective hands. Exhaling, bend the right knee and pull the right foot as close to the right ear as possible. Ensure that the left leg remains stretched straight on the floor and the big toe gripped firmly by the left hand. Sit as upright as possible. Fix the gaze on the left toes or ahead. Hold the posture still for a few comfortable seconds, whilst focusing the mind on the body and the breath.

3. On exhalation, straighten and lower the right leg to the floor by bending forward. Release the toes and relax. Repeat by bending the left leg.

Koormasana

कूर्मासन

Koorma means tortoise.

Benefits

The spine is fully stretched, exercising the whole back and pelvis. All the organs are most beneficially worked on. Such a strong stretch in the back leaves one feeling totally renewed, refreshed, revitalized and relaxed. The practice of this asana develops concentration, quietness, steadiness, wisdom, determination, patience and perseverance.

Method

1. Sit firmly upright on the floor with the legs about a foot and a half apart to the front.

2. Bend the legs in, join the soles of the feet together and form a diamond shape with the legs nearer to the trunk. Bend forward from the hips and slide the right hand under the right calf near the ankle, and the left hand under the left calf near the ankle, with the palms turned up. Extend the trunk further forward and push the whole of the right arm under the right knee bringing the right shoulder close to the right knee. Likewise, push the left arm under the left knee, bringing the left shoulder close to the left knee. Keeping both the arms and the palms facing up, while adjusting the trunk and the arms on exhalation, extend the forward stretch further. The arms should now be almost fully out from under the legs. Bend the arms and place the hands, one on top of the other around the toes. Cup the toes firmly with the hands and exhaling, pull the trunk forward as much as you comfortably can. Rest the forehead on the feet. Close the eyes and remain still and relaxed.

3. Release the hands and whilst keeping the arms under the legs, spread and stretch them out to their respective sides with the arms and palms facing down. Twist the arms out with the thumbs down first, so that the palms are facing up. Take the arms right back and grip the fingers firmly at the back. With the head still resting on the feet, adjust and accommodate the body firmly and comfortably in between the legs. Remain still and relaxed in the posture, breathing normally and concentrating on the knotted asana.

4. Release the hands, spread the legs about 1.5 feet to 2 feet apart, and stretch the arms behind keeping the palms turned up. Push the trunk further forward, straighten the legs as much as possible and rest the forehead on the floor. Adjust, and fit yourself firmly and comfortably into Koormasana. Quietly observe and enjoy the meeting of the body, mind and breath.

5. Untwist and face down the arms and palms, and slide and return them outstretched to the front. Lift the head and on inhalation, raise the trunk by drawing the arms out from under the legs. Relax.

Malasana

मालासन

Mala means garland.

Benefits

Malasana tones the muscles and joints of the limbs, pelvis and back. The abdomen and the chest are also strongly worked on. Women suffering from irregular periods may find this posture beneficial. The posture works on the heart, lungs, digestive organs, intestines and bladder, improving their functions. It breaks down energy blockages, particularly in the lower abdomen, pelvis and lower back, and it increases blood circulation. It has a soothing, relaxing effect on the nerves. Like mala (garland), the body is wrapped in the arms. Mother earth is humbly touched by the forehead, making this a strong surrendering posture of yoga. Physical and mental rest and vitality are experienced.

Method

1. Squat on the floor with the feet flat and together.

2. Keeping the feet flat and together throughout, separate the knees approximately shoulder width apart. Cup the armpits over the knees and place the palms on the floor in front of the feet. Spread the knees out still further, and bend forward from the hips by pushing the trunk and arms in between the spreading legs. On exhalation, press the feet into the ground and further bend forward by spreading the legs further and lowering and pushing the trunk and arms further in between. Wrap the arms, one at a time, round the bent legs and back until the hands are able to grip the ankles/heels or clasp each other at the back. Adjust to make the body as comfortable as possible. Lengthen the back and the neck and rest the forehead on the floor. Breathe naturally, maintain stillness and focus consciously on the Malasana with the eyes either closed or gazing at the floor.

3. On inhalation, raise the head and release the hands. Bring the arms forward and raise the trunk. Resume the sitting posture. Straighten the legs and relax.

Siddhasana

सिद्धासन

Siddha means sage – a pure being.

Benefits
This asana helps to keep the back firm, upright and relaxed. With regular practice of Siddhasana, one is able to keep a good posture even in old age. It helps relieve stiffness in the back, knees, ankles and hips. This is another posture commonly used in pranayamas, meditation and prayer. It is a much easier pose for people who find Padmasana (posture no. 71) difficult. It enables energy to travel up to the navel and heart centres, as the seat remains firmly fixed and comfortable, the spine remains upright, and the groin remains pressed in by the heel. Thus digestion and defecation is improved, backaches are relieved and concentration, wisdom, will-power, alertness and quietness are developed.

Method

1. Sit upright with the legs to the front.
2. Bend the left leg and bring the left heel nearer to the groin. Similarly, bend the right leg and place the right heel over the left ankle, with the right toes tucked between the left thigh and the left calf. Ideally both knees should touch the floor. Sit firmly and evenly on both buttocks and draw in the folded legs close to the body. Gently press in the left heel to the groin. Comfortably straighten the back from the base of the spine to the base of the skull. Gently but firmly contract the abdomen in and up. Draw the shoulders back and down, and slightly push the chest forward. Bend the arms and keep the hands on the thighs. Join the tip of the thumb and the tip of the index finger to adopt Jnana Mudra. Stretch and keep the remaining fingers together. Keep the chin parallel to the floor, the mouth, throat and tongue moist and relaxed and the lips lightly closed. Relax the face. Hold the head and the neck upright in line with the back. Close the eyes and focus the attention in between the eyebrows. Stay firm, tall, still and relaxed in the posture quietly observing the breath and the body.
3. Release and relax the fingers and legs. Repeat by crossing the legs the other way.

Padmasana

पद्मासन

Padma means lotus.
This posture is also known as Yogasana.

Hatha Pradipika says: "He who is sitting in Padmasana for pranayama is ready to become a liberated soul".

Benefits

The benefits are innumerable. A firm upright trunk gives the best support for all the systems of the body. In padmasana it is easy to keep the back upright.

It induces stillness, peace, strength, alertness and equilibrium. It has a strongly grounding, centering and uplifting effect. This asana is particularly useful for proper pranayama practice, concentration and meditation. The Prana-Shakti (life-force) can be more effectively activated, controlled and guided through the Sushumna Danda (spine) from the Mulhadara (root of the spine) to the Sahasarara (crown) Chakra by pranayamas, bandhas and mudras in Padmasana. This upright but relaxed pose develops strength and tenderness at the same time. In Padmasana a yogi is able to develop, see, feel and become the Padma (lotus flower) in Sahasarara Chakra; hence the name 'Padmasana'.

Method

1. Sit firm and upright with the legs stretched to the front.
2. Fold in the left leg and with both the hands, place the left foot with the sole turned up as high on the right thigh as possible. Fold in the right leg, and with both hands, place the right foot with the sole turned up high on the left thigh at the juncture between the abdomen and the thigh. Place the right hand on the right thigh and the left hand on the left thigh with the palms turned up. Alternatively, cup the hands on the lap in front of the abdomen, or keep the hands in Jnana Mudra on the knees with the tip of the index finger and the tip of the thumb meeting. Sit evenly and firmly on both buttocks and bring your folded legs close to your body. Keep the entire back comfortably upright. The lower abdominal muscles are gently contracted in and up, the chest is gently pushed forward and the shoulders are drawn back and relaxed. Keep the chin parallel to the floor and hold the head and neck high and in line with the spine. Keep the face soft and relaxed, and the eyes and the lips lightly closed. Keep the mouth, throat and tongue moist and relaxed. Very slightly turn up the gaze and fix the attention at the Ajna chakra (eyebrow centre). Stay firm, tall and still. Quietly meditate and relax for as long as you comfortably can in 'The posture of Yoga'.
3. Unfold the legs one at a time with the hands and relax. Repeat by crossing the legs the other way.

Note

This is an advanced yoga posture. If one is not used to sitting on the floor, the body will feel rigid at first. In these circumstances, one should start by first sitting in Sukhasana (posture no. 2), then progress to Ardha (half) Padmasana by taking one leg up on the opposite thigh as above. In the beginning, a cushion could be used to support the spine. With perseverance and daily disciplined practice of other yoga asanas together with this posture, one should be able comfortably to extend the time spent in this posture.

Padma Parvatasana

पद्म पर्वतासन

**Padma means lotus.
Parvata means mountain.**

Benefits

As well as all the benefits of Padmasana, in this asana the breathing becomes fuller. The lungs, heart, arms, back, shoulders, wrists and fingers are exercised and toned. Tendons and ligaments are kept strong. The thyroid and parathyroid glands are also stimulated. Concentration, will-power, stillness of body and mind are experienced and developed in this asana. One feels calm, energetic and centred after its practice.

Method

1. Sit in Padmasana (posture no. 71).
2. Interlock the fingers firmly, and whilst inhaling, stretch the arms above the head and turn the palms up. Gently push the chest forward and draw the shoulders as far back as possible so that the arms are in line with the ears. Sit firm on both buttocks, keep the back erect, abdomen drawn in and up, and the chin parallel to the floor. Fix the gaze ahead at eye level or close the eyes. Breathe naturally, hold the posture steady for a comfortable period and relax as much as possible.
3. On exhalation, lower the arms and release the hands. Unfold the legs and relax.
4. Repeat by changing the crossing of the legs.

Note

For variation, practise in Vajrasana (posture no. 47) or in Virasana (posture no. 48).

Vajrasana   **Virasana**

Tolangulasana

तोलङ्गुलासन

Tolangula means a scale, to balance.

Benefits
The hips, stomach and the back, particularly the lumbar and cervical regions are strengthened in this pose. The navel area is contracted and energized. A balancing pose, Tolangulasana helps develop physical and mental strength, focus, body-mind co-ordination, balance and confidence.

Method

1. Sit in Padmasana (posture no. 71).
2. On exhalation, lean back whilst raising the folded legs off the floor, stretch the arms to the front at shoulder-level with the palms facing each other and balance the body on the hips. Keep the gaze fixed ahead and keep the pose steady for a few comfortable seconds breathing normally.
3. Lower the folded legs to the floor and straighten the body to resume the sitting Padmasana pose. Unfold the legs one at a time with the hands and relax. Repeat by crossing the legs the other way.

Yogamudrasana

योगमुद्रासन

Yoga means union with the Self.
Mudra means expression.

Benefits
The hips, spine, pelvic floor, arms, hands and legs get an excellent workout. This posture aids the digestive organs, improves breathing and circulation. The crossing of the arms at the back strengthens the chest, lungs, arms, shoulders, elbows and wrists. A good posture for anxious, hyperactive and sensitive people. Stretching, bending and relaxing forward in this advanced posture works on the heart, throat and forehead centres. It creates a harmonious connection between thought, speech and actions. Memory, will-power, intelligence and humility are developed.

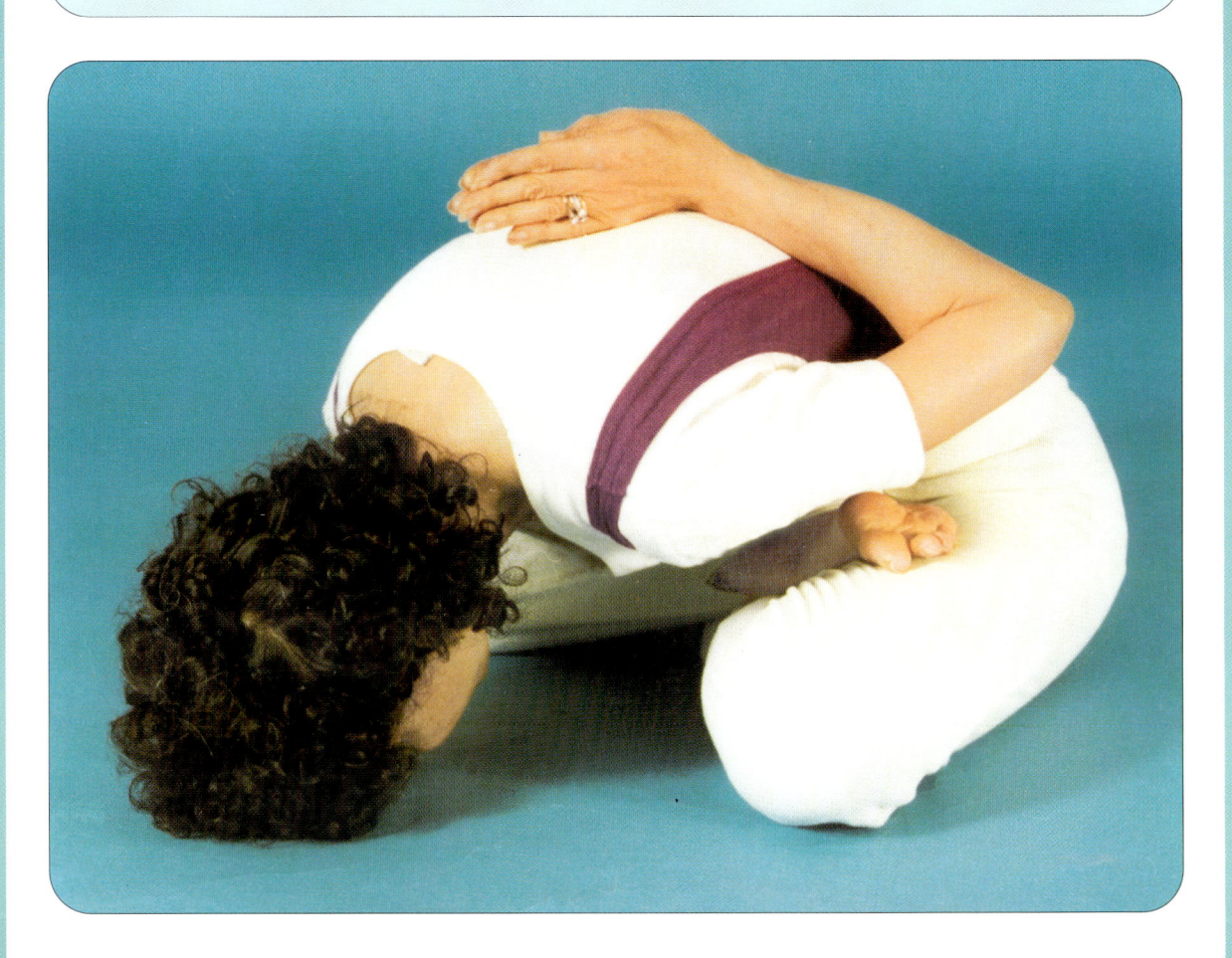

Method

1. Sit in Padmasana (posture no. 71).

2. Take both arms behind the body, twist them out and join the palms together as in prayer. Push the enjoined palms up behind the heart. Inhaling deeply, draw the shoulders back and down and push the chest to the front. Sit firm, even and tall on the buttocks. Whilst exhaling, steadily bend forward from the hips and place the forehead on the floor. Adjust the shoulders, arms and hands and stay firmly seated on the floor. You may close the eyes if you wish. Relax as much as possible.

3. On inhaling, turn the face to the front and raise the trunk. Release the hands and arms, unfold the legs and relax. Repeat by crossing the legs the other way.

Padma Matsyasana

पद्म मत्स्यासन

**Padma means lotus.
Matsya means fish.**

Benefits

Padma Matsyasana strengthens the entire spine and helps keep the back supple and pain-free. Circulation in the back, chest, abdomen, hips, legs, throat, face and head is improved. It gives relief from constipation, piles, gas and flatulence and is a good posture for diabetics and asthmatics. The nerves are strengthened and soothed and the mind and breath are calmed. The stretch in the knees, thighs and pelvis is intensified in this supine Padmasana. The chest is pushed up and expanded, improving the function of the lungs and heart. The asana helps to improve the workings of the uterus, bladder and intestines. The general posture is improved with the regular practice of Padma Matsyasana. One feels refreshed, calm and confident.

Method

1. Sit in Padmasana (posture no. 71).

2. Place the palms flat on the floor with the fingers pointing to the buttocks, about 6" behind the hips and 6" apart. Bending the elbows, gradually lean back. While continuing to recline the back, lift the hands off the ground one at a time and place the elbows on the floor in the same spot. Arch the back and neck and place the crown of the head on the floor. Stretch the arms beside the body with the palms turned up. The body is now supported by the head, hips and the folded legs. The chin is pointed up and the eyes are closed. Breathing naturally and keeping the mind focused on the body and the breath, stay still in the posture for a few seconds.

3. Bend the elbows, hold the hips from the back with the hands and press the elbows onto the ground and straighten the back and head on the floor. Grip the toes with the hands, close the eyes and relax the body and the breath.

4. On inhalation, stretch the arms and hands over the head with the palms turned up. Keep the arms close to the head. Close the eyes and be still in the posture, allowing the breath to flow naturally. Quietly observe the body and the breath.

5. Bend the elbows and join the palms together either just above the head or on the heart, as in prayer. Breathe normally, close the eyes and stay still in the posture. Focus the attention on the posture.

6. Grip the hips from the back with the hands, anchor the elbows on the floor near the hips and raise the body back into Padmasana. Unfold the legs and relax. Repeat by crossing the legs the other way.

Note

As this is a strong posture, one should take care and listen to the body carefully when practising it. Ideally, learn it under supervision.

75

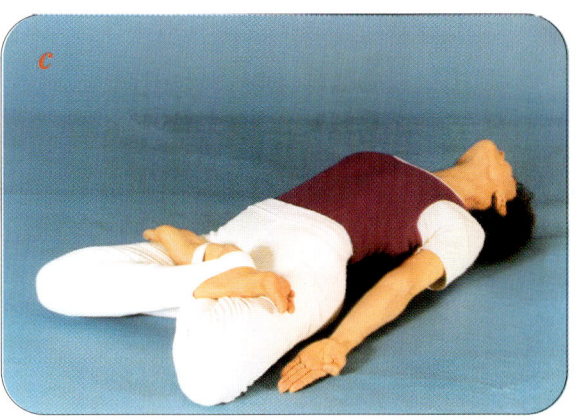

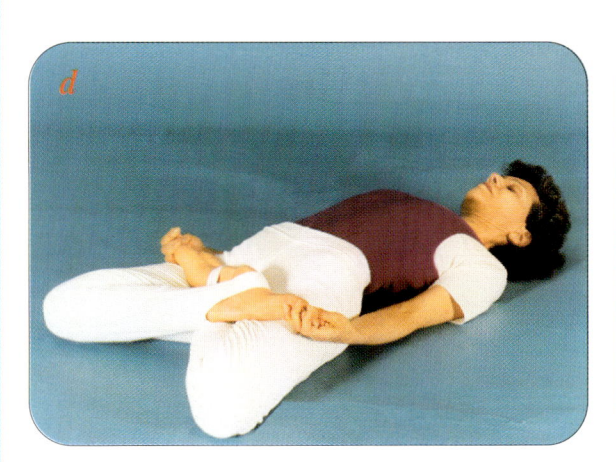

Padma Simhasana

पद्म सिंहासन

Padma means lotus.
Simha means lion.

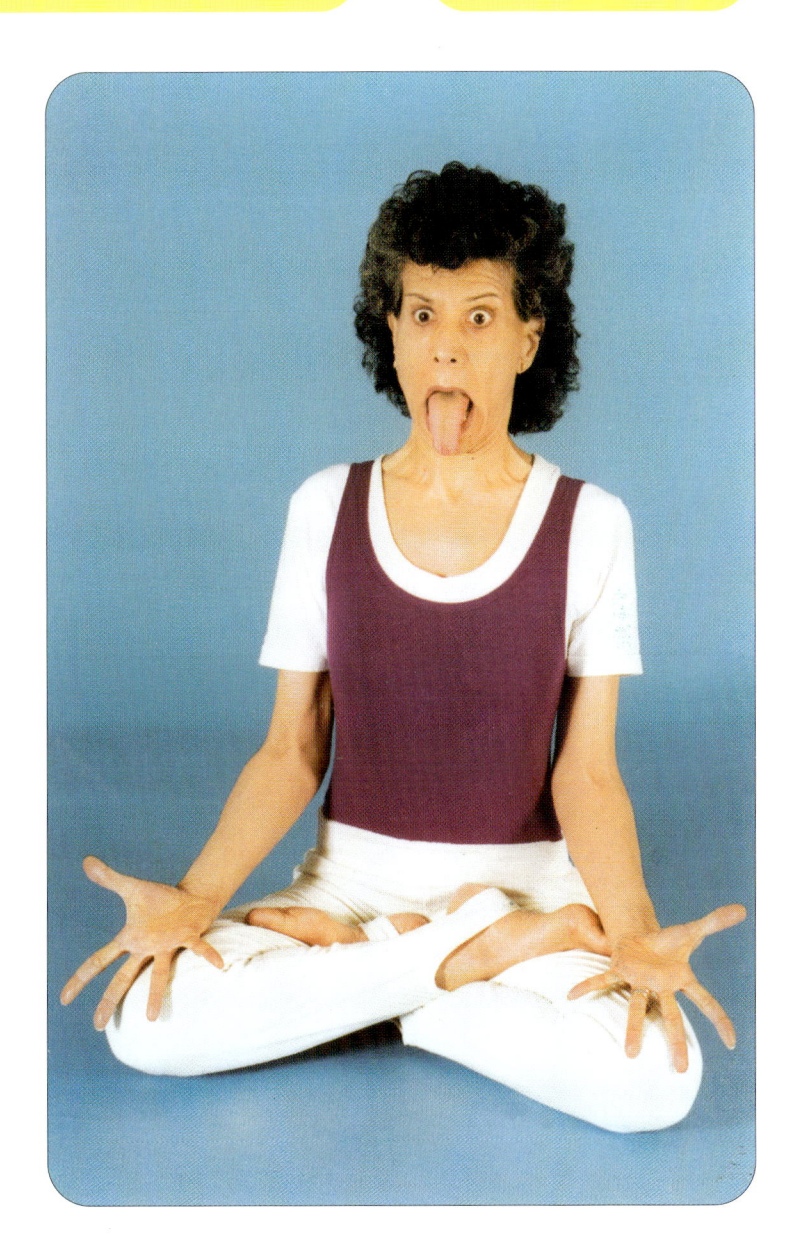

Benefits

Simhasana is excellent for the sinuses and facial tensions. By opening energy channels in the head, neck and face, and by improving blood circulation in these areas, headaches are relieved and a youthful appearance is retained. Voice production and breathing ability are improved and one can expect a decrease in stammering. The muscles in the face, neck, arms, hands, eyes, throat, ears, mouth and tongue are toned. It clears the head, develops will-power, positive thinking and concentration, bringing physical and mental strength, rest and refreshment.

Method

1. Sit in Padmasana (posture no. 71).
2. On forcefully exhaling, open the mouth wide, stretch the tongue out and down, and at the same time open the eyes wide and stretch the palms and spread the fingers. Fix the gaze and attention up at Kutastha centre (between the eyebrows) or straight ahead. Hold the out-breath and the posture steady for a few seconds.
3. Withdraw the tongue, close the mouth and the eyes, relax the mouth, throat, face and hands and let the breathing come back to normal. Repeat when ready.

Bhujanga Padma Simhasana

Bhujanga means cobra.
Padma means lotus.
Simha means lion.

भूजंग पद्म सिंहासन

Benefits

In Bhujangpadma Simhasana, all the spinal and other joints and muscles are strongly worked on, which helps to keep the back and the body strong and supple. The chest is expanded, strengthening the lungs and increasing breathing capacity and circulation. Arms, legs, shoulders, knees, back, ankles and wrists are strongly exercised. This vitalizes all the systems of the body. This asana is good for stammering and improving the voice. It is also very beneficial for the sinuses. The muscles in the face, neck, arms, hands, eyes, throat, ears, mouth and tongue are exercised and relaxed. It is an excellent asana for restoring respiratory health. It helps develop will-power, positive thinking and concentration. It helps undo physical and mental stress knots, and clears the head which brings physical and mental rest, stability and strength. At the end of the lion's ferocious force, its opposite of peace and calmness are experienced. The benefits listed under Padma Simhasana (posture no. 76) are intensified in this posture.

Method

1. Sit in Padmasana (posture no. 71).

2. Press the fists onto the floor near the hips, raise the hips off the floor and bring the body onto the knees. Lean and bend forward from the hips and place the palms on the floor about 15" in front of the knees with the fingers pointing to the front. Walk the hands forward, one at a time, whilst at the same time arching the back and sliding the body ahead until you are able to comfortably balance the body on the hands and knees. Bend the arms, arch the back further and as evenly as you can by pushing the pelvis down and raising the head up. Draw the shoulders back and down. When the body is firmly established in this posture, open the mouth wide on forceful exhalation and stretch the tongue out and down. Open the eyes wide and fix the gaze ahead. Fix the attention at the Kutastha centre (between the eyebrows) or straight ahead. Remain in this posture for a few comfortable seconds.

3. Draw the tongue in and close the mouth and eyes. Press the palms onto the floor and inhaling, raise the body, arch out the back and sit back in Padmasana. Unfold the Padmasana one leg at a time with the hands and relax. Enjoy the cool, refreshed feeling in the mouth. Repeat by crossing the legs the other way.

Note

This is a strong posture which ought to be practised carefully and learned under guidance.

Lolasana

लोलासन

Lola means swing.

Benefits
This asana exercises the back, arms, hands, legs and abdominal muscles, and almost all the joints. It helps strengthen the abdominal organs, bladder and lungs improving digestion, elimination, respiration and circulation. It helps develop will-power, patience and physical-mental poise and confidence. When the mind is focused and the hands (actions) are grounded, life flows comfortably and weightlessly.

Method

1. Sit in Padmasana (posture no. 71).
2. Place the palms flat on the floor beside the hips. Press them firmly onto the ground and on inhalation, raise the seat and the folded legs off the floor. Adjust by straightening the trunk as much as possible, balancing the weight firmly on both hands. Swing back and forth, and stay for a few seconds or more, according to your ability.
3. On exhalation, lower the body to the floor, uncross the legs and relax. Repeat by crossing the legs the other way.

Note
Another strenuous posture. Care must be taken and it must be learned under supervision.

Kukkutasana I

कुक्कुटासन १

Kukkuta means cockerel or hen.

Benefits
Besides the benefits of Padmasana, this asana strengthens the back, arms, shoulders, elbows, wrists, chest and abdominal muscles. The practice of Kukkutasana improves digestion, elimination, circulation of blood, respiration, and bladder and kidney functions. It also improves concentration, body-mind co-ordination and develops will-power.

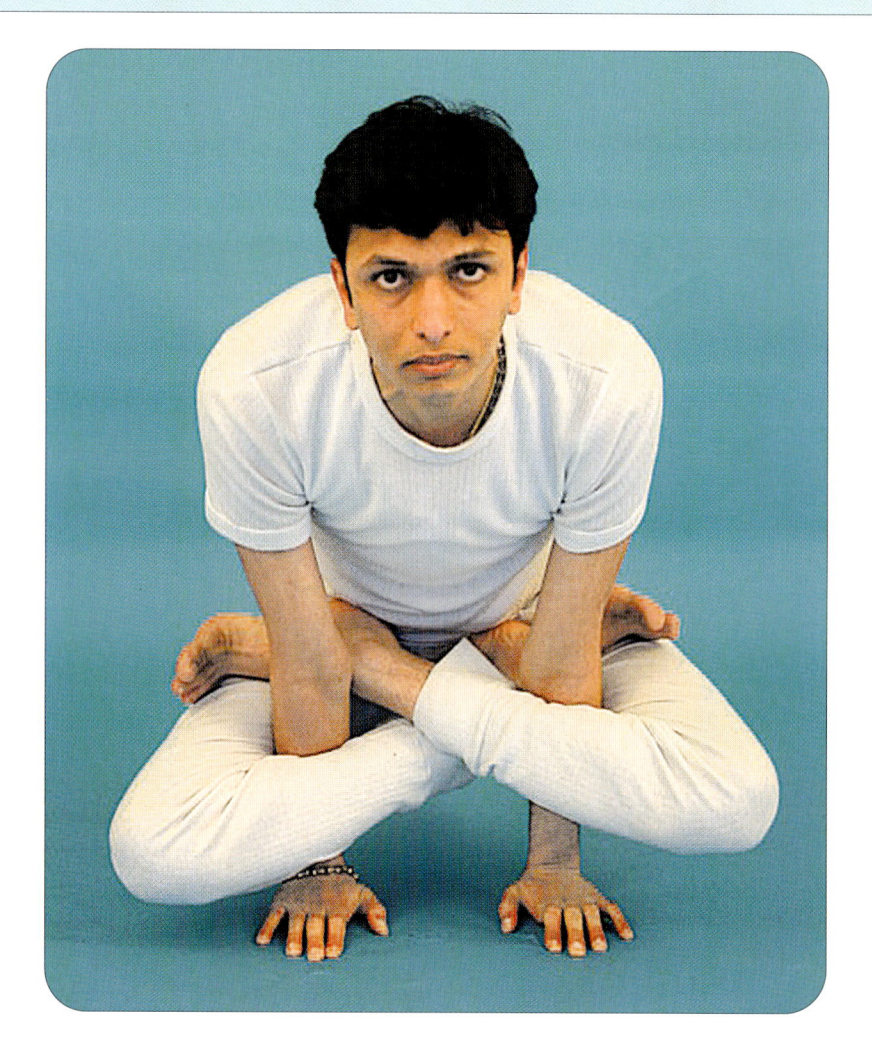

Method

1. Sit in Padmasana (posture no. 71).
2. Push both the arms, one at a time in the space between the calf and the thigh on their respective sides. Spread the palms and the fingers out on the floor, press them in firmly and evenly, and inhaling raise the body off the floor, balancing it on the hands. Keep the back as upright as possible and hold the posture steady for a few seconds.
3. On exhalation, lower the body and bend the arms. Draw them out one at a time. Unfold the legs with the hands and relax.
4. Repeat by crossing the legs the other way.

Note
Kukkuta is very strenuous on the back and the wrists. It should be learnt under supervision and tackled with care and within one's ability.

Deepasana

दीपासन

Deep means flame.

Benefits

This posture strengthens the digestive organs, the bladder, uterus, abdomen, pelvis, chest and lungs. Ligaments, joints, tendons and nerves are strengthened, particularly in the arms, legs and back. This asana is a good corrective for drooping shoulders and/or rounded shoulders. Will-power, concentration and balance are developed in the pose. One feels refreshed and energised.

Method

1. Squat on the toes with the knees wide apart, the soles of the feet almost facing each other and the heels as much together as possible.
2. Inhaling, stretch the arms over the head, twist them out and join the twisted palms together. Adjust and balance the body firmly on the toes without putting the weight on the heels. Keep the back upright, the knees and the seat raised and the toes firmly tucked. Open out and broaden the chest and draw the shoulders back so that the arms are in line with the ears. Fix the gaze ahead. Stay steady in this balancing posture for a short period breathing normally. Keep the mind focused and relaxed.
3. On exhalation, untwist and lower the arms. Bring the knees together and lower them and the heels to the ground. Sit and straighten the legs and relax.

Naukasana I   नौकासन १

Nauka means boat.

> **Benefits**
> Naukasana strengthens the abdomen, back, chest, pelvis, legs, arms, hips, neck and shoulders. The posture reduces bulge around the abdomen, hips and the waist. It develops physical and mental strength, co-ordination and focus.

Method 1

1. Sit in Dandasana (posture no. 46).
2. Breathe in and on exhaling, recline the trunk and at the same time raise the legs off the floor with the toes pointing up to the ceiling. Simultaneously, raise the arms keeping them parallel to the floor at shoulder-level with the palms facing each other. Keep the arms, legs and palms stretched all the time and hold the breath at the end of the exhalation. Balancing on the buttocks and looking to the front, stay steady and focused in this demanding posture.
3. Lower the body gently to the floor and relax. You will automatically inhale a deep satisfying breath. Let the breathing and your body's rhythm settle down.

Method 2

1. Lie down on the back with the legs straight and stretched together, and the arms stretched close to the body with the stretched hands facing the thighs.
2. Breathe in, and on exhalation, raise the trunk, stretch legs and arms in the shape of a boat (as above) and balance the body on the buttocks. Hold the breath at the end of the exhalation. Adjust so that the legs remain stretched together, the heels remain pushed away, the toes remain pointed up and the arms remain stretched together and parallel to the floor and at shoulder-level with the palms facing each other. Balance strongly and steadily on the buttocks for a few seconds looking ahead. Remain silently aware of the posture.
3. Lower the body gently to the floor and let the body and the breath be free and relaxed.

Naukasana II   नौकासन २

Nauka means boat.

Benefits
Naukasana strengthens the abdomen, back, chest, pelvis, legs, arms, hips, neck and shoulders. The posture reduces bulge around the abdomen, hips and the waist. It develops physical and mental strength, co-ordination and focus.

Method 1

1. Lie flat on the back with the legs stretched together and the hands interlocked under the head.
2. On exhalation, raise simultaneously the legs, trunk, arms and the head and balance the body on the buttocks. Hold the out-breath. Keep the legs stretched together with the heels pushed away and the toes pointed up. Keep the elbows drawn back and the hands firmly interlocked behind the head. Hold this strong posture steady and still with the eyes fixed ahead for a comfortable period.
3. Inhaling deeply, lower the body to the ground. Relax.

Method 2

1. Sit in Dandasana (posture no. 46).
2. Interlock the fingers firmly and place the hands behind the head. On exhalation, recline the trunk and simultaneously raise the stretched legs balancing the body on the buttocks. Keep the legs stretched together with the toes pointed up, heels pushed away and the elbows drawn back. Without breathing in, steady the posture on the buttocks with the eyes fixed ahead for a few seconds.
3. Inhaling deeply, lower the body to the ground. Relax.

Vishishthasana

विशिष्ठासन

Vishishtha was a great sage and this asana is named after him.

Benefits

This asana strengthens the back, wrists, arms, neck, shoulders, hips, legs, ankles, feet, lungs, abdomen and heart. Although it emphasises the sides of the body, the whole body and all the systems benefit from this strong, balancing pose. Will-power, steadiness and poise are developed. Through this posture, one learns to hold oneself strong in trying and difficult situations.

Method

1. Sit on the floor and roll on to the left hip and leg. Keeping the left arm stretched, place the left palm with the fingers pointing away from the hips, flat on the floor and in line with the left hip and under the left shoulder. Keep the legs stretched together and in line with the left hip.

2. Whilst inhaling, press the left hand onto the ground and lift the body, balancing it on the feet and the left hand. At the same time stretch the legs and place the right foot flat on the floor in front of the left foot. Adjust to make the body as straight and streamlined as possible to balance the weight firmly and evenly on the left hand and the feet. On inhalation, stretch the right arm straight up and in line with the left arm with the right palm facing the front and the fingers pointed up. Slightly push the chest and the collar bones to the front. Turn the face to the front and fix the gaze ahead. Remain steady and focused in this strong balancing posture for a few comfortable seconds. Breathe normally and relax.

3. On exhalation, lower the right arm, bend the knees and the left elbow and carefully lower the body and relax. Repeat on the other side when ready.

Bakasana

बकासन

Baka means crane.

Benefits

An excellent asana for strengthening and relaxing the entire body, particularly the neck, arms, legs, hips, wrists, chest, back and abdominal muscles. Circulation of blood is increased, particularly in the chest, upper back, neck, abdomen and the head area. Memory, clarity of thoughts, intelligence, will-power, peace of mind and balance are developed in this inverted posture. The nervous system is vitalized and relaxed. One feels totally rejuvenated and refreshed.

Method

1. Sit in Vajrasana (posture no. 47).
2. Slightly bend forward and place the palms on the floor roughly 8" in front of the knees, and about 12" apart. Putting the weight on the hands and knees, raise the seat and bend forward. Bend the elbows, tuck the toes in and lower the head to the floor. Raise and place the left knee on the upper left arm, close to the elbow still keeping the tips of the toes on the floor. By gently pressing the tips of the left toes onto the ground, raise and place the right knee on the upper right arm close to the elbow. Raise first the left and then the right foot completely off the floor. Smartly and carefully, draw the folded legs and the stretched feet up. Straighten the inverted trunk by raising the hips up and by further pulling in the folded legs and the feet. Balance the body mainly on the arms and very slightly on the head. Remain firm, steady and still for a few seconds.
3. Carefully lower the legs and resume the beginning posture. Relax.

Note

Proper care ought to be taken when practising this posture. It is advisable to learn it from an expert and it should be mastered gradually with patience.

Kukkutasana II

कुक्कुटासन २

Kukkuta means cockerel or hen.

Benefits

The arms, wrists, elbows, shoulders, hips, back, knees, legs and abdomen are exercised and strengthened in Kukkutasana. This is another whole body posture. All systems of the body benefit from the practice of this asana. It particularly eases the flow of the fresh blood to the chest, head and neck area, and venous blood to the heart. It brings steadiness, strength, co-ordination and control in the body and the mind. One feels totally energised and relaxed.

Method

1. Squat with the feet slightly apart and flat on the floor.
2. Spread the knees about 12" apart and place the armpits over the knees with the palms on the floor about 12" apart and about 15" in front of the feet. Bend the elbows and at the same time raise the hips and the heels. Press the palms firmly onto the floor and lean forward. Balancing the weight on the hands and the left toes, raise and place the right knee on the back of the upper right arm near to the bent elbow. Cleverly and carefully, place the left knee on the back of the upper left arm. Straighten and bend the inverted trunk and the head forward and down, by raising the hips and the legs up, and by pulling the feet in and up together. Breathing naturally, remain in the posture for a short comfortable period.
3. Carefully, gently and smartly lower the tail and bring the feet down one at a time to resume the squatting posture. Straighten the legs and relax. Let the breathing and the body's rhythm settle down.

Note

Extra care should be taken when practising this advanced asana.

Mayurasana   मयूरासन

Mayur means peacock.

Benefits

An excellent asana for digestive disorders. Due to the pressure applied on the abdomen, the abdominal organs are immensely strengthened aiding digestion and detoxification. Blood circulation and breathing ability are improved. Arms, wrists, hands, elbows, shoulders, legs, back and hips are strengthened. This asana develops physical and mental strength, balance, and co-ordination. Strength, courage, calmness, confidence and concentration are required, and are further developed in the practice of this pose.

Method

1. Kneel with toes tucked onto the mat and the knees approximately 6" apart.
2. Bend forward, place the hands about 12" in front of the knees turned out and round so that the fingers are pointing towards the knees. The little fingers of the hands, and both the arms are touching each other in the centre. Bend the elbows, press the palms firmly and evenly in and rest the abdomen against the joined steady elbows, the diaphragm on the elbows and the chest on the back of the upper arms. Avoid putting pressure on the ribcage. Stretch back one leg at a time, then, keeping them both together, balance the abdomen on the elbows and the upper arms. Press the palms firmly in and steadily, smartly and confidently raise the stretched legs together or one at a time in line with the trunk and the head. Extend the trunk and the head. Hold the posture steady for a comfortable period.
3. Lower the legs to the ground. Bend the knees, lift and lower the seat, lift and untwist the arms and relax.

Note

It is best to take expert advice before commencing the practice of this advanced asana.

Padangusthasana

पादांगुष्ठासन

**Pada means feet/legs.
Angustha means toes.**

Benefits
This asana is excellent for strengthening and maintaining flexibility in all parts of the lower body. It relieves stiffness in the back and weakness in the abdominal organs. When the body is so firmly and evenly balanced and upright, the mind automatically becomes strong and steady and focuses with ease. One is better able to concentrate and relax at will.

Method

1. Keeping the legs slightly apart, squat on the toes.

2. Balance the body-weight on the left leg, carefully lift the right leg with both hands, twist it and place the upturned right foot high on the left thigh. Remain firm and erect on the left toes. Join the palms together in front of the chest as in prayer and fix the gaze ahead at eye level. Breathe naturally and stay steady and relaxed in the posture.

3. Using the hands carefully and smartly bring the right leg down and resume the squatting pose. Lower the heels and the buttocks to the floor, straighten the legs and relax. After a short rest repeat on the other side.

Vatayanasana
वातायनासन

Vata means air.   Vatayana means horse – one that moves swiftly like wind.

Benefits
Vatayanasana keeps all the spinal joints and muscles in good condition, ensuring strength and mobility in the sacro-lumbar region, pelvic floor and legs. Nerves are strengthened and will-power, concentration and patience are developed. A strong horse-like, mobile body and a controlled quick mind are attained. Physical and mental strength, speed and agility are possible through regular practice of Vatayanasana.

Method

1. Sit on the floor in half Padmasana (posture no. 71) with the left foot placed high on the right thigh and the sole turned up.

2. Whilst in the folded position, bend the right knee and place the right foot flat on the floor near the right hip. Press the fingers onto the floor near the hips, and whilst turning the left leg on to its knee, raise the seat and bend forward. Adjust, to keep the left knee and the right foot in line and about 10" away from each other. Straighten the seat, raise the trunk and slightly straighten the right leg. Balance the body on the left knee and firmly press the right foot in. Fold the hands in prayer position and fix the gaze ahead. Hold for a short comfortable count and breathe as it comes.

3. For a variation, bend the elbows a little and place the right upper arm on the left upper arm. Entwine them around each other and join the palms together as in prayer. Bend the elbows further and draw the entwined arms close to the chest (or to the right). Adjust by straightening the back and balancing the posture as much as possible. Breathe normally, gaze ahead and hold firmly for a comfortable period. Focus the mind on the body and the breath, and relax.

4. Release the arms and lower the seat carefully and gently to the floor. Unfold the legs and relax. Repeat on the other side.

Note

Patience, care and perseverance are needed to master this pose. It is important that the posture is first learnt and practised under supervision.

Ardha Chakrasana

अर्ध चक्रासन

Ardha means half. Chakra means wheel.

Benefits

Innumerable benefits could be achieved with a regular and proper practice of Chakrasana. It keeps the spine and limbs very strong and flexible, even in old age. It tones and soothes the nerves and improves the circulation of blood in the whole body. It improves digestion and helps relieve constipation, gas, flatulence, piles and fistula. Intense and full opening in the rib cage tones the entire chest, improving lung capacity. The sense organs, i.e., the skin, sense of smell, voice, hearing and eyesight are all improved. Circulation to the brain improves. The whole body and mind benefit immensely from this great posture. Intelligence, calmness, memory, attentiveness, will-power and concentration are developed.

Method

1. Lie on the back with the legs together.
2. Bend the knees and draw the feet close to the hips. Raise the arms over the head, bend the elbows and place the palms on the floor, with the fingers together and pointed towards the feet under the shoulders. Firmly press the feet and palms onto the floor, raise the trunk and exhaling, curve the back in a deep and even upward bend. Balance the body firmly on the feet and palms. Press the palms and feet firmly again, stretch the arms and legs as much as possible, let the neck and the head relax between the arms and whilst exhaling, open and arch the back to its maximum. Breathe normally and remain still and comfortable in the posture for a short period.
3. Resume the lying down pose by bending the elbows and knees, and gradually lowering the body.

Note

Purna (full) Chakrasana can be undertaken by advanced practitioners by carefully walking the feet and the hands to each other under the body, in order to grip the feet with the hands to form a wheel. As the posture is very strenuous, it should be learnt gradually and under supervision, taking extreme care as mishaps can sometimes lead to sprains, dislocations and even fractures.

Sarvangasana

सर्वाङ्गासन

Sarva means all.
Anga means body parts.

Benefits

Among many of its innumerable benefits, this asana improves blood circulation, aids digestive and defecation organs, strengthens the bladder and the reproductive organs. It stimulates the thyroid and parathyroid glands. It allows the venous blood to flow more easily from the hips, legs and abdomen to the heart and the fresh blood from the heart to the neck and head. The back, hips, legs and feet are relieved of body weight and are thus energised and relaxed. As all the internal organs and body systems are turned upside down, they get a chance to adjust better and work more efficiently and in harmony. This posture gives strength and vitality to the whole body and mind. Creativity, wisdom, memory, calmness, intelligence and will-power are developed.

Method

1. Lie flat on the back with the legs stretched together.

2. Bend the legs and bring the knees onto the abdomen. Press the palms onto the floor beside the hips, raise the hips and the folded legs and place the hands on the hips and the elbows on the floor, to support the body. On exhalation, raise the trunk further by turning the hips in and up, and give support by moving the hands higher up the back. Keep the knees bent and straighten the back until it is vertical to the floor, the knees are lightly touching the forehead and the chest is closer to the chin. Keeping the legs together, straighten and stretch them up, to bring them in line with the trunk. Stretch the feet and point the toes. Adjust the pose so as to avoid any pressure on the throat, and at the same time, adjust without straining, the back and the legs to be as perpendicular to the floor as possible. Close the eyes and focus on the posture for a short period.

3. Bend the legs and lower the knees to the forehead. Gradually and patiently lower the body to the floor by sliding the hands down the back and the hips taking care not to pull or jerk the neck. Straighten the legs and relax in the Shavasana (posture no. 1).

Note

With sufficient practice one can easily increase the staying time in this pose. It is not advisable to practise this asana during menstruation or if you suffer from high blood pressure, headaches or other head, neck, heart, eyes or breathing problems. Seek advice if in doubt.

Eka Pada Sarvangasana

Eka means one.
Pada means legs/feet.
Sarva means all.
Anga means parts.

एक पद सर्वाङ्गासन

Benefits

As well as the benefits listed under Sarvangasana (posture no. 90), this vigorous sequence is particularly helpful for abdominal and back complaints. All the systems of the body and mind gain in strength, flexibility and the free flow of energy and calm.

Method

1. Assume Sarvangasana (posture no. 90).
2. On exhaling, lower the left leg straight over the head. Keep the leg stretched and the toes to the floor. Breathe normally and stay firm and relaxed in the posture for a few seconds.
3. On inhalation, raise the left leg and stretch it up in line with the right leg.
4. Follow steps 2 and 3 with the opposite leg.
5. On exhalation, bend the knees down to the forehead. Keeping the hands on the back, turn them so that the fingers and thumbs are pointing out and the wrists are pointed in. Tilt and lower the bent legs from the hips in the opposite direction i.e. away from the head by arching the back. Continue arching the back and lowering the legs until the feet are down on the floor as in Setuasana (posture no. 35). Keep the feet firm and flat and hip-width apart and the knees bent. Adjust the arch and support the back properly by pushing the back up and pulling the elbows in and anchoring them properly well under the bridge.
6. Stretch the right leg straight up and balance the weight on the elbows, shoulders, head and the bent left leg and foot. Keep the sole of the right foot parallel to the ceiling and the toes pointed ahead and the heel pushed away and up. Breathe normally and stay steady for a short period.
7. On exhalation, lower and bend the right leg and bring the right foot to its original place in Setuasana (posture no. 35). Adjust to stay firm in the posture.
8. Stretch the left leg straight up and repeat the posture on this side as in step number 6 above.
9. On exhalation, lower and bend the left leg and bring the left foot to the floor in its original place in Setuasana (posture no. 35). Adjust the back.
10. Lower the arms beside the body and gradually lower the back. Massage the back by rubbing it against the ground and relax.

Setu Sarvangasana

सेतु सर्वाङ्गासन

Setu means bridge.
Sarva means all.
Anga means parts.

Benefits

There are innumerable benefits of this asana. Besides all the benefits of Setuasana (posture no. 35), the intensified working of the spine makes the entire back strong and flexible. Circulation, digestion and breathing improve. This posture will energize the nervous system. It is excellent for the whole body and mind. One feels calm, controlled, refreshed and revitalized and experiences deep sleep-like rest.

Method

1. Assume Sarvangasana (posture no. 90).

2. On exhalation, bend the knees down to the forehead. Keeping the hands firmly on the back, turn them so that the fingers and thumbs are pointing out and the wrists are pointing in. At the same time, tilt and lower down the bent legs from the hips in the opposite direction, i.e. away from the head. Carefully continue arching the back and lowering the legs until the feet are down on the floor as in Setuasana (posture no. 35). Keep them firm and flat and hip-width apart. Keep the knees bent. Adjust and support the posture by pushing the back further up, by arching it in evenly, by wedging the elbows properly under the bridge and by pressing the feet and the elbows firmly in. The body is now in Setuasana. Breathe as it comes, close the eyes and enjoy this semi inverted posture. Remain as still and relaxed as possible.

3. Stretch the legs to the front one at a time. Keep the soles of the feet as much on the ground as possible. Push the elbows firmly in and lift the head and tilt it back until the crown rests on the floor. Close the eyes and relax in this most energising and yet most calming posture.

4. Straighten the neck and the head, bend the knees and draw the feet closer to the hips one at a time. Adjust the body once more in the supported Setuasana.

5. Stretch the left leg to the front, place the left heel on the ground and point the toes up. Similarly stretch the right leg to the front and cross the right ankle over the left ankle. Lift the head, turn and tilt it as far back as possible to rest the crown on the floor. Close the eyes and remain still in the posture.

6. Straighten and rest the neck and the head. Uncross the legs and drawing the feet to the hips, bend the knees one at a time. Keep the feet flat in their original place in the Setuasana (posture no. 35). Lower the arms beside the body and exhaling, lower the back gradually to the ground. Massage the back by rubbing it against the ground and relax.

Note

This is an advanced posture. Learn with care, patience and thought and work within your ability.

92

Padma Sarvangasana

पद्म सर्वाङ्गासन

Padma means lotus.
Sarva means all.
Anga means parts.

Benefits

This series of asanas give intense backward, forward, lateral and twisting movements to the spine, thus balancing and strengthening the entire back. All the muscles and joints are toned. All the organs are exercised, stimulated and massaged, helping them to function at their best. Peristaltic movements are increased, digestion and elimination are improved. Gas, dyspepsia and constipation are relieved. Breathing, blood circulation, bladder and kidney functions are improved. The nervous system is nourished. The sequence has a grounding effect on the body and mind. When the head and neck are so closely, and for so long, pressed to the earth, and when all the chakras are worked on, the best human qualities like mindfulness, attentiveness, patience, understanding, will-power, quietness, memory, wisdom, intelligence, love etc., are developed. It is the most rejuvenating and refreshing sequence of yoga.

Method

1. Sit in Padmasana (posture no. 71).

2. Place the palms with the fingers pointing to the buttocks on the floor behind the body, 6" away from the hips and 6" apart. Bending the elbows and gradually lowering the back, lift the hands one at a time and place the elbows on the ground. Supporting the body with the elbows and the hands, lower the back and the head to the floor. Withdraw the arms one at a time and lay the back on the floor. Straighten the arms beside the body. Press the palms onto the floor beside the hips, raise the folded legs (the padma) at right angles to the trunk, and inhaling, raise the hips, the padma and the back off the floor, simultaneously supporting the back by placing the hands on the hips and the elbows on the floor. Supporting the back by moving the hands up to the middle back, further raise the trunk. Gradually straighten it until the back is almost perpendicular to the floor, with the padma still at right angles to the trunk. Straighten the padma, point the knees to the ceiling and bring the padma and hips in line with the back. Adjust to avoid discomfort to the throat. If you wish, you may close the eyes and stay in the posture. Breathe normally and focus the mind on the body and the breath.

3. On exhalation, lower the padma by bending forward from the hips to bring the knees to the head. Rest the knees on either side of the head. Adjust to avoid discomfort to the throat caused by the pressure of the posture. Close the eyes and breathe naturally. Relax in the posture for a short period.

4. Raise the folded padma a little, and on exhalation, twist and lower the padma as far to the left of the head as possible. Make sure to keep the hands, elbows, shoulders and head in the same place. Adjust to avoid pressure on the throat. Close the eyes and remain still in the posture. Watch the breath and the posture.

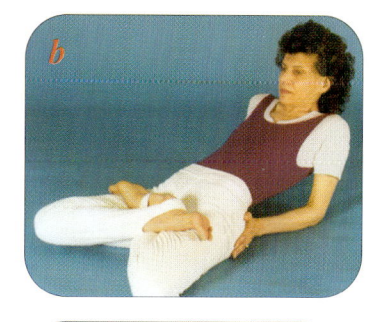

5. On exhalation, bring the bent padma back to the centre. Adjust to centre the body, and on the next exhalation, twist the trunk and lower the padma to the right side of the head. Close the eyes and remain still. Watch the breath and the posture.

6. On exhalation, bring the knees back to the forehead. Adjust to centre the body. Lower and stretch the arms behind the back and firmly interlock the hands. Breathe naturally, relax in the pose and focus the attention on the body.

7. Release the hands. On inhalation, stretch the arms over the head and fold them round the head. Adjust to avoid any pressure on the throat. Remain quiet whilst breathing normally and relaxing in the posture.

8. Unfold the arms and once again support the back by bringing the hands on the back and the elbows on the ground. Straighten the padma, the hips and the back, and point the knees to the ceiling. Exhaling, arch the lower back and slightly lower the padma in the opposite direction i.e. away from the head by turning the hands on the back to point the fingers and thumbs out and the wrists in. Adjust and support the body firmly. On exhalation, continue to arch the back and lower the padma a little further. Take extra care as the movement in this direction is very limited. Breathe normally and stay in the posture for a few seconds.

9. Bring the body back to the centre. Lower the padma by bringing the knees to the forehead.

10. Exhaling, lower and ease the back and the padma carefully and gradually to the ground by sliding the hands over the buttocks. Make sure you do not pull or jerk the neck. Grip the hips from behind with the hands, press the forearms and elbows on the floor and sit back into Padmasana. Unfold the legs with the hands and relax. Repeat by crossing the legs the other way.

Note

Great care must be taken when one decides to practise this demanding sequence.

Halasana

हलासन

Hala means plough.

Benefits

The benefits are innumerable. Halasana exercises and tones the muscles and joints of the entire body. There is improvement in the circulation, particularly in the arms, abdomen, back, lower limbs and in the head, shoulder and neck area which facilitates a youthful appearance.

By increasing thyroid activity, the sequence is useful to help reduce weight, particularly around the hips, abdomen and waist.

Constipation, gas and other minor digestive and abdominal complaints are helped by this sequence. The stretch in the spine and neck, tones and relaxes the nervous system. It is a whole body posture. Energy channels are opened and the body is bathed in vitality, creativity and calmness. The voice becomes peaceful, clear and pleasant to hear after this sequence. Clarity of thought is achieved, memory is sharpened and buddhi (wisdom), memory and intelligence are awakened. One feels renewed, totally refreshed and alert after its practice. In this asana the legs and feet are taken to where the head is, as if ploughing the mind to find the essence of life and to walk and act according to the dictates of the Self.

Method

1. Assume Sarvangasana (posture no. 90).
2. On exhalation, bend forward from the hips and stretch the legs over the head. Adjust the shoulders, the back of the neck and the back, to keep the back as perpendicular to the floor as possible. Take care not to put suffocating pressure on the throat or the lungs. Close the eyes and remain still and relaxed in this pose for a comfortable period. Observe the breath and the posture. Stretch the arms on the floor behind the back with the palms turned down. Interlock the hands. Adjust the back, the shoulders and the neck to help the hips to tilt forward more and the legs to stretch more fully. Unlock the fingers and stretch the arms with the palms turned down and stretched on the floor. Close the eyes and relax. Quietly observe the breath and the posture.
3. On inhalation, take the arms over the head and stretch them and the hands turned up in line with the legs. Stay firm and relaxed in this most mind engrossing variation of Halasana. Remain aware of the breath and the body.

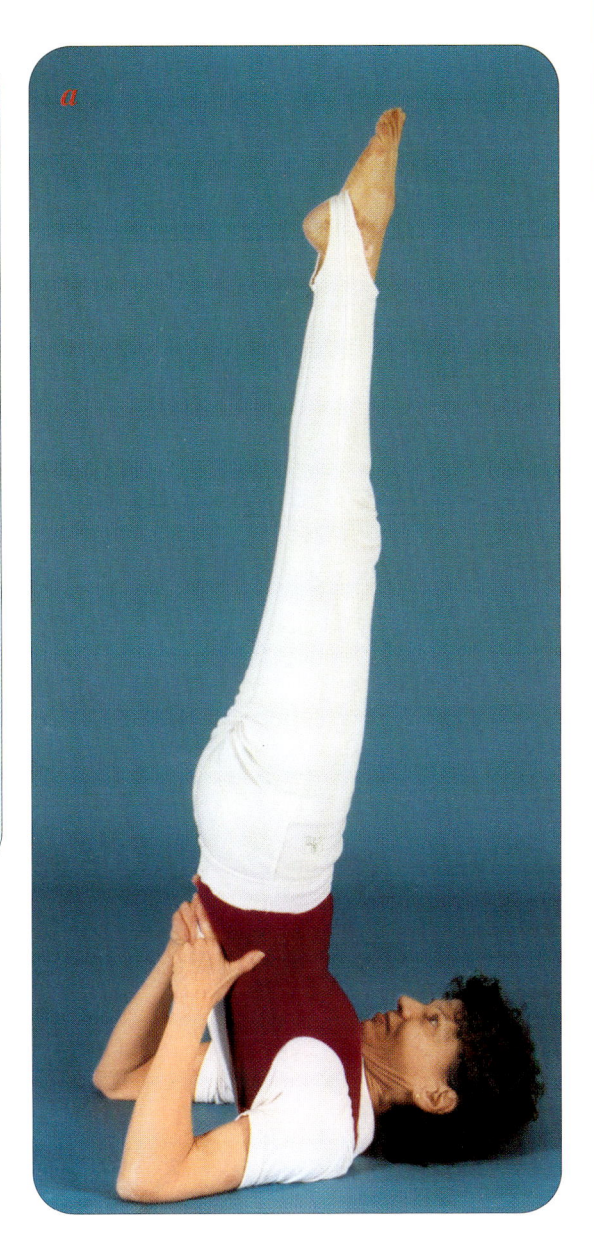

Karna Pidasana

**Karna means ear.
Pida means weight/pressure/pain.**

4. On exhaling, take the arms behind the back and support the back with the hands as before. Bend the legs so that the right knee is next to the right ear and the left knee is next to the left ear. Take the arms up and over and wrap them round the back of the legs. Stay still and relaxed in the posture, observing the breath and the posture. Lower the arms on the floor behind the back. Interlock the fingers and adjust the shoulders, the neck and the back. Release the hands, bend the arms and support the back once again with the hands. Adjust and stretch the legs and tuck the toes in properly to get ready for the following posture.

Parsva Halasana

Parsva means side of the body.

5. On exhaling, walk both legs one foot at a time, as far to the right as possible without straining or disturbing the position of the shoulders, upper back, neck, or the head. Adjust the hold by stretching and keeping the legs together, and by supporting the trunk properly with the hands. Close the eyes and remain still and relaxed in the posture for a short comfortable period.
6. On exhaling, walk the legs back, one at a time, to the centre so they are in the original position in line with the head. On the next exhalation, similarly walk them as far to the left as possible without straining or disturbing the position of the upper back, shoulders, neck or head. Adjust and remain still in the posture for a comfortable count, concentrating on the breathing rhythm and the posture.
7. On exhalation, walk the legs back to the centre in line with the head. Adjust and support the back properly again with the hands.

Suptakonasana

**Supta means supine.
Kona means angle.**

8. On exhalation, walk and spread the stretched legs as far apart from each other as possible in their respective directions. Hold the toes with their respective hands. Adjust the body and fix yourself properly in the posture. Close the eyes and remain still and relaxed according to your ability in this wonderful posture. Quietly concentrate on the posture and the breath.

9. Release the toes and bend the arms once again to support the back with the hands. On exhalation, walk the legs back to the centre in line with the head, in the original Halasana posture. Bend the knees to the forehead and exhaling, carefully and gradually slide the back down to the floor by sliding the hands over the buttocks and down. Care must be taken not to jerk the neck. Straighten the legs and relax in Shavasana (posture no. 1) until the body and the breath have comfortably absorbed all the energy and the restfulness this sequence can give.

Sirsasana

शीर्षासन

Sir means head.

Benefits

This asana stimulates the blood circulation, bringing richer arterial blood to the brain which improves the functions of the brain. The adjustment of the cranial bones is facilitated. All bodily and mental systems benefit from Sirsasana, and those suffering from varicose veins, haemorrhoids, fistula, and prolapses will notice great improvement. A beginner may feel unsteady and insecure initially, but with perseverance, one will develop will-power, concentration, strength, agility, patience and intelligence needed to comfortably stay for a longer period in the posture. Initially, a short practice of Sirsasana daily will boost confidence, improve the practice and feed the desire to stay longer in the posture. The body and mind will attain and experience the most magnificent results with the regular practice of Sirsasana.

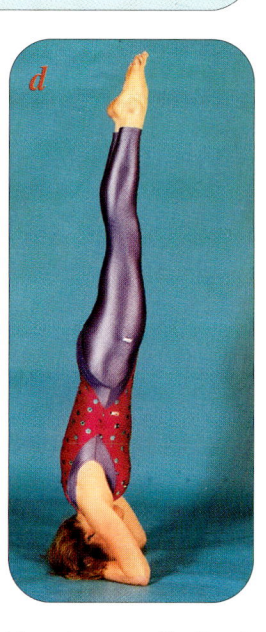

Method

1. Assume the Marijariasana (posture no. 40).

2. Bend the elbows and put them on the floor where the hands were. Interlock the fingers on the floor, place the crown on the floor in between the interlocked hands and cup the back of the head by the interlocked hands. Tuck the toes in and raise the knees off the floor. Firmly balancing on the arms and the interlocked hands, whilst raising the hips up, stretch the legs and walk the feet/toes towards the body. When you feel stable enough, press the elbows and the interlocked hands firmly onto the floor and by bending the knees, lift the feet gently but firmly off the floor. At the same time, raise the hips up further by drawing the bent legs closer to the body. Straighten the back vertically by bringing the bent knees close to the trunk. Confidently stretch up both the legs keeping them together. Stretch the feet and point the toes. Keep the whole body in a straight line. Stay relaxed in the position for a comfortable period and breathe normally. Bend the knees and gradually come down reversing the movements to sit in the kneeling posture. Unfold the legs and relax. Enjoy freshness, vitality and calmness.

Note

Beginners should learn this posture under supervision to prevent falls. If one feels hot in the face or the eyes, if there is pain in the neck or head or if the collar-bones or throat feel pressurised, then one should come out of the position and relax. If discomfort is experienced in the head, heart, chest, breathing or anywhere, abandon the practice of Sirsasana immediately and relax. Those with high or low blood pressure, or any complex or mysterious ailments should avoid this asana. It is best to consult your G.P. or a yoga teacher concerning the practice of this asana, if you have any doubts. This applies to all the postures, particularly the advanced ones.

Chandra Namaskara

चन्द्र नमस्कार

Chandra means moon. Namaskara means salutation.

Benefits
This sequence strengthens and relaxes all the joints and muscles of the body. All the systems benefit from this long, well-thought-out wave-like sequence. All the vertebrae and joints are contracted, worked on and relaxed harmoniously in a rhythm at various stages of the sequence. The mind and body are forced to release toxins and tensions and are instead nourished and relaxed. The lunar sequence is a type of moving meditation. It has a calming, cooling yet strengthening effect on all the systems of the body. Physical, spiritual and emotional well-being is experienced. Extremely relaxing when practised with soft music in the background.

Method

1. Sit in Vajrasana (posture no. 47) with the palms together in front of the heart as in prayer.
2. Raise the body on the knees with the legs together and the palms still in prayer.
3. On exhaling, step forward, with the thigh parallel to the floor, the right foot approximately 15" in the front. At the same time stretch the arms to the front with the palms together. Hold the out-breath.
4. On inhaling, stretch out the arms to the sides at shoulder level. Keep the palms face down and the fingers pointed and together. Hold the inhaled breath.
5. On exhaling, slowly and consciously rotate the trunk and the head as far to the left as possible, keeping the arms outstretched, in Ardha Chandra (half moon) formed by the arms and the rotating trunk. Hold the out-breath.
6. Deeply inhaling, slowly and consciously return to the front, and on exhaling slowly and consciously rotate the trunk and the head as far to the right as possible, keeping the arms outstretched. Hold the out-breath.
7. On inhaling, slowly and consciously untwist and return to the front.
8. Exhaling, bend the trunk and the neck down to the left. Place the left palm flat on the floor near to the left knee. At the same time stretch the right arm, keeping the fingers and thumb stretched together over the head stretching and opening the right side of the body in Ardha Chandra (half moon) formed by the right side and right arm. Look straight ahead. Hold the out-breath.
9. Deeply inhaling, raise the body and return to the centre keeping the arms outstretched to the sides. Hold the breath. Exhaling, lower the body to the right side and place the right palm flat on the floor in line with the left knee. At the same time, stretch the left arm, keeping the fingers and thumb stretched together over the head stretching and opening the left side of the trunk in Ardha Chandra (half moon), formed by the left side of the body and the left arm. Look straight ahead. Hold the out-breath.
10. Deeply inhaling, raise the body and smoothly return to the centre keeping the arms outstretched. Exhaling, lower the arms beside the body.
11. On the next inhalation, stretch the arms over the

head, draw the shoulders back, arch the back and the neck and turn the face up in Ardha Chandra (half moon) formed by the back and arms. Hold the in-breath.

12. On slow, steady exhalation, bend forward from the hips and place both the palms flat on the floor straight under the shoulders and on either side of the right foot. Keep the arms stretched and take the right leg back and place the right knee in line with the left knee and both approximately hip-width apart. Lower the head between the arms and arch out the entire back in Ardha Chandra (half moon) formed by the dome shape of the back. Hold the out-breath, in Marijariasana (posture no. 40).

13. Deeply and steadily inhaling, raise the head and the hips up, arching and concaving the entire back. Keep the arms stretched and the palms evenly and firmly rooted on the ground in Ardha Chandra (half moon) formed by the concave back in Marijariasana (posture no. 40). Hold the in-breath.

14. Draw the feet close together keeping the knees apart. Exhaling, lower the seat between the heels keeping the arms stretched and palms pressed. Place the forehead on the floor.

15. Tuck the toes in and inhaling, raise the body, balance on the toes and take and stretch the arms above the head. Spread the knees apart and sit the buttocks on the heels. Bring the arms as close to the ears as possible, draw the shoulders back and at the same time arch the back and turn the face up in Ardha Chandra (half moon) formed by the concave back and arms.

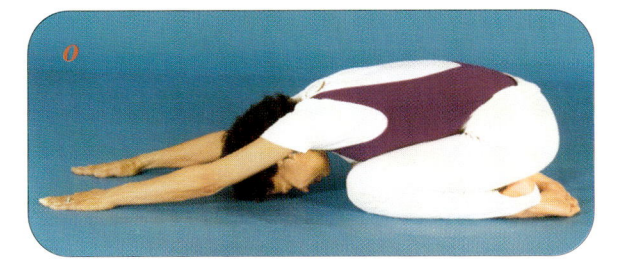

16. On exhalation, lower the heels to squat. Lower the arms. At the same time, carefully and skilfully, momentarily turn on the toes and balance on them in order to lower the knees onto the floor. Relax the feet and the toes. Sit between the heels in the starting posture of Vajrasana (posture no. 47). Join the palms in front of the heart, close the eyes and relax. Let the breathing happen naturally. Enjoy the cooling, relaxing effect of this sequence.

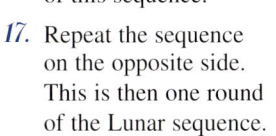

17. Repeat the sequence on the opposite side. This is then one round of the Lunar sequence.

Note

Staying-time in the posture should be adjusted according to one's ability. One can stay for a longer period and breathe normally in each taken posture in the sequence before practising the next step.

प्राणायाम

Pranayama

Prana means life • Yama means control.

Prana is the divine Spark, the very essence of the life-force. It is the intelligent, all creative energy of life. Our existence depends upon Prana.

There are five life-forces (Panch vayus). They are Prana vayu, Apana vayu, Samana vayu, Udana vayu and Vyana vayu. Prana vayu in the thorax region energises the lungs and heart. Apana vayu resides in the lower abdomen and is mainly in charge of the elimination processes, ie; gas, urine, faeces, sperm, and ovum. All the downward movements are controlled by this current. Samana vayu resides in the navel region and controls digestion. It distils prana from the food in the digestive system. Udana vayu controls the intake of food and air and works in the endocrine system. It maintains thinking and remembering processes. Vyana vayu, the last of the vayu, pervades the whole body and is responsible for distributing the energy converted from the food and air. Pranayama stimulate the life currents of these five vayus (forces) and converts them into one main life force.

The word Yama means to control. Thus the word Pranayama means to control life-force. Pranayama is a science of breath.

Most people are unaware of breath. It is accepted as a natural reflex mechanism over which they have no control. To control breath seems insignificant and unnecessary.

Respiration may be clavicular, activating mainly the upper lobes of the lungs – this is shallow breathing. It may be thoracic, activating mainly the middle parts of the lungs; this is intercostal breathing. Diaphragmatic breathing takes place in the solar plexus. It activates the lower parts of the lungs. The abdomen moves as a result of the flattening of the domed diaphragm. In pranayamic breathing, the lungs are worked to their fullest extent. Five to six times more air is inhaled compared to a normal inspiration.

The process of breathing comprises puraka (inhalation), rechaka (exhalation) and kumbhaka (suspension). The Sanskrit word puraka means to fill up, rechaka means to empty out and kumbhaka means to hold. Suspension of breath at the end of the puraka is antara (in) kumbhaka, and at the end of the rechaka is a bahiya (out) kumbhaka. Pranayama practised with a mantra is called sabija and without a mantra is called nirbija. A kumbhaka with a mantra is a sagarbha kumbhaka and one without a mantra is an agarbha kumbhaka. A highly advanced yogi is able to practise kumbhaka after puraka and/or rechaka for a long period of time with ease and comfort.

Pranayama practice begins when one becomes aware of one's breath in asana and relaxation. A beginner usually practises breath control with some general simple breathing exercises that harmonise with his physical movements. As he progresses, he studies the natural course and rhythm of his breath and his breathing abilities. He intelligently and patiently educates himself to breathe correctly and comfortably. He learns to regulate, stabilise and anchor his breath in order to foster good health. Haste, tension or force is harmful and should never be used in training the breath. It is advisable to comfortably master the puraka (in-breath) first, and then to achieve a comfortable relaxed control over the rechaka (out-breath). By regular disciplined practice of controlled inhalations and exhalations, correct breathing becomes a habit. In the beginning, no retention should be practised until puraka and rechaka are comfortably mastered. After mastering these, retaining of the breath without tension at the end of inhalation and then at the end of exhalation is learned. Samavritta (equal duration) pranayama could easily be practised after this. In this practice we are taught to breathe in and hold the breath, and to breathe out and hold the breath – all at equal duration with counts of, for example, 5:5:5:5. The student also learns to breathe evenly steadily and deeply during Samavritta practice. Eventually through scientific pranayama a yogi channels the life force at will from the lower spinal centres to the higher centres for the transformation of his consciousness.

Calm, comfortable and steady breathing is characteristic of people whose physical and mental health is generally good. Shallow and uneven breathing is usually identified with those whose physical and mental health is not so sound. Just as restless thoughts and emotions, poor health and life-style and bad posture can cause an imbalance in the course of the breath, so controlled breathing can correct faulty thoughts, emotions and health. One's breath also reflects the state of one's consciousness. The biggest cause of restlessness on human consciousness is desire. Restlessness disturbs prana. A disturbed prana will affect one's mental and physical health. We find it hard to control our desires. By controlling prana through pranayama, we are able to control our desires. In order to achieve physical and mental health and happiness, the practice of Pranayama is most invaluable.

A dedicated and inspired beginner of pranayama is usually very eager and enthusiastic to get results. The tendency is to be impatient and harsh with oneself. Practising incorrectly, due to the lack of patience, time, knowledge and guidance is damaging. If the aspirant studies intelligently under supervision, and perseveres with patience, he will feel physically and mentally strong and calm. This will enable him to extend his practice comfortably. It will prepare him to meditate deeply and for longer periods, which in turn will enrich his life.

Pranayamic Puraka – Inhalation

At the start of the inhalation the lower abdominal muscles are gently contracted and held in and the diaphragm is lowered. This pushes the solar plexus outwards. The pranayamic inspiration lifts and expands the lower rib-cage, opens out to the front the middle intercostal area and expands the top of the ribcage and the collar-bone and sternum area. The shoulders, collarbones area, face, mouth, throat, eyes and the rest of the body are kept as relaxed as possible.

Pranayamic Kumbhaka – Retention

During puraka, the mind is guided to focus on the steady breath, its soft sound and the cool sensation. Because the breath is retained in antara kumbhaka, the mind stays focused, the chest cavity stays broad and long, and the lungs are fully stretched.

The kumbhaka should never be forced. If the rhythm of inhalations and exhalations is disturbed, the holding of the breath becomes strenuous and vice-versa.

Pranayamic Rechaka – Exhalation

At the end of the kumbhaka, without losing control of the chest or the trunk, a smooth conscious out-breath, strongly involving the lower abdominal muscles takes place. In bahiya kumbhaka, retention of breath takes place after the complete rechaka.

Pranayamas and the Systems of the Body

The eight systems of the body; nervous, endocrinal, respiratory, circulatory, digestive, skeletal, muscular and excretory, depend on each other to function efficiently. Aside from directly benefiting from the pranayama, each system of the body derives indirect benefit through the better functioning of the other systems. In pranayama, the rhythmic working of the lungs, thorax and associated muscles limber, strengthen and relax the entire respiratory system and associated parts of the body. The heart is exercised and energised, ensuring a liberal supply of oxygenated blood to the body and mind. When fully expanded, the lungs send positive calming impulses to the brain. The rhythmic continuous use of the respiratory organs, diaphragm and abdominal muscles, also exert beneficial pressure on the digestive organs, in particular the liver, stomach and spleen. They are stimulated, toned and relaxed. The digestion and assimilation of food is improved, and their energetic functioning in turn accentuate the most beneficial pressure on the intestines. Absorption of the nutrients and peristaltic movements improve. Evacuation of the bowel can take place with ease. The alternating contraction and relaxation of the abdominal and associated muscles and the rise and fall of the diaphragm and connected parts, also help the functioning of the kidneys and the bladder. In one way or the other, pranayama positively affect all the organs and the systems of the body. Improved effectiveness of the immune system helps one lead a long disease-free life.

In pranayama the useless dispersal of energy due to the wayward tendencies and aimless wonderings of the mind is controlled by the fixity of attention. Mind and the senses are withdrawn from external objects and focused on the breath, the body and the peace experienced in pranayama. The mind is refreshed. It is clear, calm and alert. The high pressure induced in the central canal of the spinal cord by bandhas (locks) and mudras (expressions) in pranayama, develop energy circuits in the body and mind and access one's deeper physical, psychic and spiritual realms that replenish the whole nervous system and the body with vitality and bounce. The positive pressure on the endocrinal glands causes efficient working of the endocrine system. This positively affects not only the physiology, but also the psychology of an individual.

Pranayama Practice
Time and Place
The best time for yoga is first thing in the morning when the stomach is empty and the body and mind are rested and receptive. After attending to the bowel and bladder, and bathing, and before breakfast, start the pranayama. It is best to precede pranayama with a session of asana. Yoga nidra (relaxation), dharana (concentration) and dhyana (meditation) are easier after pranayama.

Pranayama Posture

Any of the following postures are good for pranayama: Siddhasana (posture no. 70), Padmasana (posture no. 71), Vajrasana (posture no. 47) or Sukhasana (posture no 2). If sitting on the floor in any of the postures is difficult, you may sit on a chair, away from the back rest with the feet flat and comfortable on a blanket on the floor.

Sitting in Sukhasana (sukha means peace, happiness, comfort), the most common of all the meditation postures, spread the weight firmly and evenly on both buttocks and fold the legs comfortably and firmly as close to the body as you can. Keep the back comfortably erect from the base of the spine to the base of the skull. Draw the abdomen slightly in and up without tensing or holding the breath. Slightly open out the chest and draw the shoulders and collar bones back and down. Relax the arms and place the relaxed upturned palms on the thighs or on the lap. At the same time, consciously straighten and yet relax the back. Keep the chin parallel to the ground and stretch the back of the neck by lifting the crown of the head and drawing in the chin. Keep the neck and head upright and in line with the spine. Relax the mouth and the throat and create more room in the mouth. Keep the tongue and lower jaw relaxed. Keep the face soft and relaxed. Close the lips lightly. Keep the eyes lightly closed throughout the practice to invite rest and to avoid distractions. Turn the gaze slightly up to the Kutastha centre (between the eyebrows) without tensing. Be sure to sit firm, well anchored, tall and yet relaxed all the time.

Points to Remember

After the pranayama, either sit silently, with the eyes closed or lie down in Shavasana (posture no. 1).

Pranayamas generally take a long time to master. They should be practised calmly with ease, care, patience, attention, intelligence and awareness.

Faulty practice can have adverse effects on the body and the mind. It can cause irritation and straining of the head and eyes, and aches and pains in the ears and head. It can irritate and strain the whole nervous system and may cause dizziness, nose bleeding, restlessness, fidgeting and loss of memory. Remember that it is not the quantity of air inhaled in puraka, and the length of retention in kumbhaka, or the quantity of air exhaled in rechaka, that is important in pranayama, but the quality of the inhalation, retention and exhalation. Forced and unnatural holding of the breath and forcefully breathing longer and deeper than is comfortable, can create disorders. Unnatural pressure on the lungs and the diaphragm may damage them. This in turn could affect all the systems of the body. If forceful inharmonious practice prevails for a longer period, it can cause irreparable damage to the nervous system. It could cause nervous breakdown or even death.

People suffering from any heart, chest or lung ailments, blood disorders, headaches, dizziness, complaints of the eyes, ears, head, nose, throat, and people who have a weak constitution or who are ill, must check with their yoga teacher or doctor before starting on a disciplined pranayama programme. People with high or low blood pressure and those who are not generally well, who are convalescing or who are beginners and those who have doubts should not practise suspension of the breath.

If, instead of feeling refreshed and calm, you easily get angry and remain restless or nervous after pranayama, or if you are in any doubt whether you should practise a certain pranayama, or if you need to verify the details, it is best to check with the teacher. If no guidance is available, wait until you are sure of what you are doing.

If pranayama practice depresses you or makes you feel low and introverted, practise more asana and less or no pranayama for a period of time. Try later on and see how you feel. Once again, have your practice checked. Relaxation is the basis and the ultimate aim of pranayama. We should never waver from this aim by allowing our enthusiasm, eagerness, impatience or competitiveness to get the better of reason in pranayama practice or in the practice of any ashtanga.

Pranayama is a tool that is guaranteed to help if practiced correctly.

There are eight scientific pranayamas mentioned in yoga text. They are: 1) Ujjayi, 2) Surya Bhedana, 3) Nadi Shudhana, 4) Kapalabhati (is also a cleansing kriya), 5) Bhastrika, 6) Sitali, 7) Sitakari and 8) Bhramari.

1. UJJAYI

Method

1. Sit firm and tall but relaxed in a pranayama posture. With eyes closed, observe the breathing.
2. Breathe out completely. Partly close the glottis, and slightly contract the abdominal muscles. Breathe in deeply and steadily through the nostrils. This partial closing of the glottis will produce a continuous smooth sound in the throat as the air smoothly and softly rubs against the roof of the mouth.
3. Close the glottis completely and take the Jalandhara bandha (see Bandha and Mudra) by contracting the pharynx. Practise the kumbhaka (retention of breath) for a short comfortable count.
4. Unlock the Jalandhara bandha and partially open the glottis. Breathe out slowly and steadily through the nose, without causing tension, and simultaneously relax the thorax gradually. The abdominal contraction gets stronger in the process. The out breath is heard in a smooth continuous pitch as the air smoothly and softly rubs against the roof of the mouth.

Repeat a few times for 5 to 7 minutes. Relax and breathe normally.

This completes one round of Ujjayi.

Take care not to tense whilst practising Ujjayi. The muscles in the nose should not be contracted. If tension is felt whilst either holding, inhaling or exhaling, know that you are working or holding beyond your capacity. This is not advisable. Make sure to end the out-breath without straining. If the out-breath is not smooth, relaxed and longer than the inhalation, then you were holding for a period beyond your lungs' capacity at the end of the in-breath. If the following inhalation is not better than, or at least as comfortable and smooth as the first one, then you must cut down on your kumbhaka (holding) time. Every rechaka (exhalation), puraka (inhalation) and kumbhaka is practised with ease for each pranayama to be successful. If in doubt, check with your teacher.

Benefits

Ujjayi energizes all the systems, particularly the lungs and abdomen. It soothes the nerves and calms the mind. Concentration is enhanced.

2. SURYA BHEDANA

Surya means sun. Bhedana means to pierce. In Yoga, the right nostril is the Surya Nadi (sun channel) and the left nostril is the Chandra Nadi (moon channel).

Method

Sit tall, firm and relaxed in a pranayama posture. Close the eyes and observe the breath.

Bend the right arm and bring the right hand close to the nose. Place the tip of the index finger and the middle finger on the Ajna centre between the eyebrows. Place the little finger and the ring finger near to the left nostril and the thumb near to the right nostril. (See Nadi Shudhana).

Press the left nostril in with the ring finger and the little finger below the nasal bone and breathe out completely from the right nostril. Press the lower part of the right nostril slightly with the thumb. Inhale deeply and steadily through the partially blocked right nostril. At the end of the inhalation block the right nostril completely by pressing below the nasal bone with the thumb. With both nostrils blocked, take the Jalandhara bandha by contracting and bending the neck forward, and resting the chin on the chest between the collarbones and above the breastbone. Retain the breath and hold the bandha for a few comfortable seconds. Lift the head, release the Jalandhara bandha, unblock the left nostril and start exhaling through it steadily.

This is one round of Surya Bhedana.

Repeat a few times for 7 to 10 minutes, each time inhaling from the right and exhaling from the left nostril making sure that every inhalation and every exhalation is even and is practised with ease. Every Kumbhaka and Jalandhara bandha should be comfortable. Relax in shavasana or sit and meditate.

If any tension or dizziness is felt whilst inhaling, exhaling or holding the breath, know that you are working beyond your ability.

Remain particularly aware of the subconscious tensions caused in the body. A successful practice is signified by an even, steady, relaxed and harmonious breathing rhythm.

In Surya Bhedana, the practice of Maha bandha, i.e. Mula bandha on puraka, Jalandhara bandha on kumbhaka and the Uddiyana on the rechaka could be successively performed by an advanced pranayama practitioner.

Retention of the breath should be avoided by those who are ill or suffering from high blood pressure, by heart patients, beginners and people with a weak constitution. If in doubt, check with your teacher.

Benefits
Its practice helps clear the sinuses and head. The sinus nodes are energized and stimulated, and one feels the following in-breaths are purer and lighter. The real quality of the fresh air is felt. Senses and nerves are soothed. One's breathing capacity improves. One feels light, refreshed and revitalized. Concentration is improved.

3. NADI SHUDHANA
Nadi means channel
Shudhana means cleansing or purifying.

Method
Sit tall, firm and relaxed in a pranayama posture and observe the breath.

Bend the right arm and draw the right hand close to the nose. Place the tip of the index finger and the middle finger on the eyebrow centre (Ajna centre). Place the little and the ring finger near to the left nostril and the thumb near to the right nostril.

Press firmly yet comfortably on the left nostril with the ring finger and the little finger below the nasal bone. Breathe out completely through the right nostril.

Inhale deeply and steadily through the right nostril. Block the right nostril firmly yet comfortably with the thumb below the nasal bone. In this way both the nostrils are blocked firmly and the breath is retained.

Apply the Jalandhara bandha by contracting and bending the neck forward and resting the chin on the chest between the collarbones and above the breastbone. Retain the breath and hold the Jalandhara for a few comfortable seconds.

Lift the head, relax the Jalandhara bandha,

unblock the left nostril and start exhaling through the left nostril steadily.

Now inhale through the same nostril i.e. the left nostril deeply and steadily. At the end of the inhalation, block the left nostril with the ring and little finger below the nasal bone. Now both the nostrils are blocked. Contract the neck and throat, lower the head, resting the chin on the chest between the collar bones and above the breast bone. Hold the Jalandhara bandha for a short, comfortable period.

Lift the head, relax the Jalandhara bandha, unblock the right nostril and start exhaling through it steadily.

This is one round of Nadi Shudhana. Repeat the rounds for a comfortable period.

After the practice, lie down and relax or sit and meditate.

Every inhalation and every exhalation should be steady and deep. Throughout the practice, the breathing should be comfortable. Be aware of any subconscious tensions in the hands, throat, nostrils, as well as the body in general. Any feeling of suffocation or undue strain should not be ignored.

Retention of the breath is not advisable for those who are ill, or who suffer from high blood pressure, heart patients, beginners or people with a weak constitution. If in any doubt check with your teacher.

Benefits
The air feels purer and cooler after Nadi Shudhana as the channels are cleared and stimulated. The practice helps to clear the sinuses and head. The mind is calmer and one feels lighter and refreshed. It has a vitalizing and soothing effect on all the systems of the body.

4. KAPALABHATI

Kapala means skull. Bhati means a fire or to shine.
Kapalabhati is predominantly an abdominal breathing exercise. It is also a cleansing technique.

Method
Sit tall, firm and relaxed in a pranayama posture. Close the eyes and observe the breathing cycle. Inhale steadily through the nose. Keep the ribs raised and the thorax contracted.

Using the abdominal muscles, expel the air with short vigorous breaths. Repeat the smooth inhalation, followed by the short vigorous out-breaths supported by the abdominal muscles. Each thrust of the out-breath is followed by a split-second retention of breath. The process continues for several rounds. At the end of the last expulsion, take a deep, steady Ujjayi breath applying the Mula bandha. At the end of the inhalation, take Jalandhara bandha for a few comfortable seconds. Lift the head, release the Jalandhar bandha, exhale as deeply and smoothly as possible with a soft sound as in Ujjayi, at the same time relaxing the thorax and releasing the Mula bandha.

This is one round of Kapalabhati. Relax and repeat the whole cycle a few more times practising Ujjayi breath in between. Relax in Shavasana.

The only muscles that move freely are the diaphragm and the front abdominal muscles. The ribs rise and fall very slightly and the thorax is relaxed only after the last round of expulsions and after the Ujjayi breath that follows the expulsions.

It is advisable that this pranayama be learnt under guidance of an experienced teacher.

5. BHASTRIKA

Bhas means to pant. Bhastrika is bellows breathing.
It is a cleansing act.

Method
The first part of Bhastrika is similar to Kapalabhati. Bhastrika is more strenuous.

Sit tall, firm and relaxed in a pranayama posture. Close the eyes and remain aware of the breath.

Breathe out completely. Inhale and exhale short and fast with force in rapid succession a few times. The number of expulsions are adjusted according to one's capacity. The sound is identical to the air rushing through a bellows. The end of the last expulsion is followed by a deep smooth Ujjayi in-breath. As the Ujjayi breath is inhaled the Mula bandha is applied. At the end of the inhalation, Jalandhara Bandha is applied. Both the bandha are retained for a short, comfortable period. Lift the head, release the

Jalandhara bandha, exhale as deeply and smoothly as possible with a soft low-pitch sound in Ujjayi, gradually relaxing the thorax and releasing the Mula bandha.

This is one round of Bhastrika. Relax and repeat the whole cycle a few more times according to your ability, practising Ujjayi in between.

Just like Kapalabhati, the rib cage is maintained in a raised and widened position and the muscles of the thorax are kept contracted. The only muscles that move freely are the diaphragm and front abdominal muscles. The continuous blowing through the nose and the rhythmic rise and fall of the abdominal muscles gives this pranayama its name of Bhastrika; meaning 'blacksmith's bellows'.

In another variation, inhalations and expulsions are done through one nostril at a time by blocking the other nostril with either the thumb on one side and the little and the ring finger on the other side.

Practise an even number of expulsions from each nostril. Complete the round with a round of Ujjayi breath. This is one cycle of alternate nostril Bhastrika. Repeat the cycle a few more times or according to your ability with Ujjayi breath in between.

Relax in Shavasana or meditate.

Bhastrika is more strenuous than Kapalabhati. Both these pranayama must be learnt under guidance. Beginners, people with weaker constitutions or with high/low blood pressure, low vitality, or suffering from lung, heart, ear or eye problems or from other serious illnesses should avoid these strenuous pranayamas.

Retention of breath and taking of bandha must also be avoided if you are not sure of what you are doing.

Both these pranayama vitalize and soothe the nervous and the digestive system (fire centre) in turn aiding all the systems of the body. One feels light, calm, refreshed and centered. It helps develop concentration and leads to meditation.

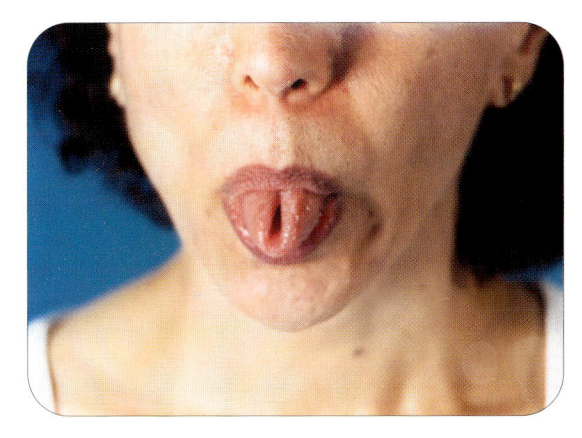

6. SITALI
Sita means cool. Ali means method.

Method
Sit erect, firm and comfortable in a pranayama posture. Close the eyes and remain aware of the breathing cycle.

Now practise the following instructions as if they form part of a single act:

Swallow and dry out the mouth. Curl the tongue lengthwise, forming a tunnel with it. Put this tunnel through the rounded lips like a tube out of a round hole. Inhale deeply and steadily through this tunnel, feeling the cool air as it brushes softly and smoothly all along the tongue on its way in. At the end of the inhalation, withdraw the tongue and close the mouth. Hold for a short time, feeling the cool sensation circulating in the mouth, throat, and in the face. Start exhaling steadily through the nose concentrating on the breath. This completes one round of Sitali. Continue without stopping for 5 to 7 minutes, depending on the ability. Relax and let normal breathing resume.

Sitali has a cooling and calming effect on the nerves, senses and all the body's systems. This is an excellent preparation for meditation.

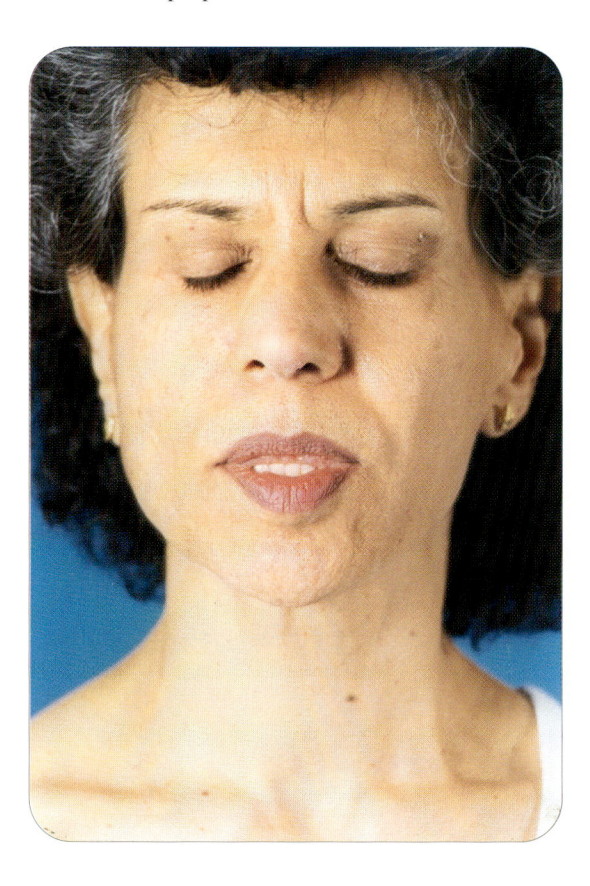

7. SITAKARI
Sita means cool. Kari means action.

Method
Sit erect, firm and comfortable in a pranayama posture. Close the eyes and observe the breath. Swallow and dry out the mouth. Breathe out completely through the mouth. Keep the mouth slightly open. Lower and push forward the lower jaw. Press the tip of the tongue to the back of the lower incisors. Keep the tongue as flat as possible. Suck in the air slowly, steadily and continuously on inhalation. A smooth hissing sound is made and a sweet coolness is felt as the air brushes against the tongue and the roof of the mouth on its way to the throat. Concentrate on the hissing sound and the cool air. At the end of the inhalation, hold the breath, withdraw the tongue and close the mouth. Concentrate on the cool sensation felt in the mouth, throat and face. Hold for a few seconds according to your ability. Start exhaling consciously and steadily through the nose. Practise this pranayama for 5 to 7 minutes continuously in one sitting and then relax, letting the normal breathing resume.

Benefits are similar to the practice of Sitali.

Both Sitali and Sitakari should be learnt under supervision. Retention of the breath should be within the limits of one's ability, or avoided if in any doubt. This pranayama will prepare you for concentration and meditation.

8. BHRAMARI
Bhramari means bee.

Method
Sit tall, firm and relaxed in a pranayama posture. Close the eyes and observe the breath. Inhale deeply. Start exhaling slowly under control through the nose making a continuous lower pitch nasal sound of 'nnnn'. Inhale forcefully and steadily through the nose making a high, smooth and prolonged sound of 'nnn' with the soft palate. This is one round of Bhramari. Practise successive rounds in a stretch for 5 to 7 minutes or more in one sitting, concentrating on hearing the sweet humming sound. Relax in Shavasana (posture no. l) or sit and meditate. Bhramari develops concentration and calmness and leads to successful dhyana (meditation).

In the beginning, the sound may be rough and irregular but with practice it will become smooth, sweet and sonorous. The sound is the main part of this pranayama. The mind becomes concentrated on the soothing sound and the pleasurable sensation that is felt. This is a most beneficial pranayama for sinus sufferers. It helps alleviate nervousness, restlessness and fickle-mindedness. One feels light and refreshed after its practice. The voice becomes gentle and soothing. The throat, lungs and abdominal muscles are strengthened. Like all other pranayama, this one should be learnt under supervision over a period of time until good control is achieved over the sound.

Pratyahara

Pratya means towards • Hara means moving

Pratyahara, the fifth limb of ashtanga is a process which checks the outgoing power of the mind and turns it inwards. Pranayama together with Pratyahara constitute a bridge between asana, the physical outer limb of ashtanga and dharana and dhyana, the inner limbs of ashtanga.

At the pratyahara stage, one makes a conscious effort to focus on various mind control techniques. Initially, the familiar lighter techniques, ie: music, colour, mantras, chants, mandalas, visualization, breath and affirmations are used to calm the mind. It is then focused on inner sounds, such as the soft breath and the rhythmic beats of the heart. The energy is conserved and guided on its inner journey by advanced meditation techniques (raja-yoga). The harmonious musical sounds of the chakras along the spine neutralise and silence the internal physical sensations and thoughts. A yogi withdraws the life force completely from the sense nerves and retires in his mind. His mind becomes engrossed in Itself. Although he may experience input from the senses, his mind is not affected. The self merges into the Self and the transformation of a yogi's consciousness takes place.

धारणा

Dharana

Dharana means to focus the mind on a certain thought/object. We may make use of mantra, breath, mandala, colour, music, visualizations, affirmations and prayer amongst other beneficial influences to guide our thoughts in one direction.

When we succeed in focusing attention for a period of time at one sitting, then the image starts to take shape. It eventually becomes sharp, clear and three dimensional. During this process, some unwanted thoughts automatically drop away through lack of attention. More stubborn thoughts need to be dealt with wisely. As one progresses, one is more able to control one's thoughts.

It is advisable not to exclusively concentrate on getting rid of unwanted thoughts as this may entrench the very thoughts we are trying to remove. It is very important to remain positive and concentrate on the intended goal.

The upright yet relaxed posture of Padmasana (posture no. 71) reflects the meditator's disciplined yet relaxed efforts to attain his goal.

ध्यान

Dhyana

*"The lake must always be still,
though people may swim,
and may even throw rocks,
the lake must always be still."*

In our everyday life, the word dhyana signifies that we carry out our tasks with loving care and thoughtful attention.

As we progress in our yoga practice, we realise that meditation implies a single-minded focusing on one concept with intelligence and devotion.

Dharana, Dhyana and Samadhi are three ascending degrees of concentration. Each merges into the other. The fine line between them is defined by the meditating individual according to his level of understanding. Once a yogi's mind is focused on a concept, he makes the effort to meditate at a deeper level and for a longer time, until his individual mind merges into the Universal mind, and until the meditator, the object of his focus and the process of meditation become one. During the processes of concentration, the disturbances caused by extraneous noises; by thoughts, breath, rhythms of heartbeat and blood circulation can be controlled by rhythmic, smooth chanting, suitable music, pranayamas and sounds of chakras, etc. An effort is made to create the right quality and quantity of pressure on the chakras (energy wheels) and nadis (energy channels). In this way, a transformation of a yogi's consciousness takes place.

Dhyana is usually practised in the quiet of the early hours of the morning, after attending to the requirements of bladder and bowel, and before breakfast. Allow three hours gap after a main meal and about an hour's gap after a light meal. The most beneficial and favourable times are:

1. Early morning, when it is neither dark nor light.
2. At 12 noon – midday, when the sun is at its peak and the day's energy is most intense.
3. In the late afternoon, when the daylight is turning into night.
4. At midnight, in the pitch dark, when the night is at its peak.

However, one can meditate anywhere and at anytime of the day and night.

Choose a quiet, clean, unspoilt place in the open or in a room with ventilation. For increased benefit, use the same place and keep the same time for meditation. For ease, practise asana and pranyama before meditation. In the eastern tradition, one faces the east to meditate. Sit on a mat or on a folded blanket either in Siddhasana (posture no.70) or Padmasana (posture no.71) or Vajrasana (posture no.47) or Sukhasana (posture no.2). You may sit on a chair keeping the back upright and away from the back rest, and the feet flat and comfortable on a blanket on the floor.

Sit comfortably in Sukhasana, the most commonly used meditation posture. Put the weight evenly and firmly on both buttocks. Firmly but comfortably, fold and draw the legs close to the body. At the same time, consciously align the back from the base of the spine to the base of the skull. Without tensing, slightly draw the abdomen in and up, and open the chest outwardly and to the front. At the same time draw the shoulders slightly back and comfortably lower them. Relax the arms and place the upturned palms either one cupped in the other on the lap, or individually on each thigh. Keep the chin parallel to the ground and hold the neck and the head upright and in line with the spine. Create more room in the throat and mouth by relaxing the tongue, mouth and throat and by moistening the mouth. Relax the face and the forehead. Keep the lips and eyes lightly closed throughout the practice. Comfortably turn the gaze very slightly up to the kutastha centre (eyebrow centre). Make sure you sit firm, tall, well-balanced and well-anchored, and yet relaxed all the time.

The benefits of meditation are innumerable. It would be impossible to list them all.

By strengthening a yogi's body, mind and inner being, and by reducing the wear and tear of the body and mind, meditation fosters good health and happiness and lengthens one's life. The development of intuition, peace, clarity of thoughts and calmness, heightens a yogi's awareness of the falsity and subtlety of the most enticing and intricate power of maya (cosmic delusion). He develops the power to use the delusion positively for his own growth. He is able to develop ways to achieve well-being and happiness for himself and others.

Meditation is our own personal and direct contact with the Self. Since the positive attributes of life easily and spontaneously germinate and take root in the fertile and receptive mind of the yogi, the Creator is able to reveal and impart his hidden omnipresent, omniscient and omnipotent nature to him. A yogi becomes a creator of his own destiny. Meditation, together with other ashtanga, fulfils man's greatest need and deepest desire of Peace – 'union with the Self'.

Meditating in the disciplined upright yet relaxed Padmasana (posture No.71), a yogi becomes strong and malleable like molten metal. He is not easily overcome by the trials of life. He remains untainted by the duality of maya as the lotus remains untainted by the muddy water.

Samadhi

*Sama means balanced, even, calm, tranquil.
Adhi means state of consciousness.*

Profound shanti (silence), bliss, intense love and deep joy are experienced by a deeply meditating yogi. In the state of samadhi, a yogi frees himself from the limited individual mind. He merges into the eternity from whence he came. No words can describe his joy. Having once tasted the union with the Self, he is forever in love with it.

Ashtanga begins with the disciplines of Yama and Niyama (control). These uproot bad habits and establish moral and spiritual values in one's life. In the beginning one may find it difficult to implement yama and niyama disciplines. Therefore many people begin their yog-sadhana with the easier bahir angas (outer limbs) i.e. Asana and Pranayama.

Asana help to attain physical fitness and mental strength, calmness and control. Pranayama strengthen the body and mind and initiate the process of pratyahara. Pratyahara neutralises the movements of the thoughts and emotions by turning the mind within. By sitting still and silent in dharana and dhyana, a yogi becomes a master of himself. Finally in Samadhi, the mind merges into Mind. The Self speaks silently and clearly to the intuitive ear. This way, the path that begins with the Disciplines of yama ends with Freedom in samadhi.

Sitting in samadhi in Padma (lotus), a yogi becomes That. He is the colour, the smell, and the life. He is the seer (rishi). He is seen and he is the act of seeing. He is the omnipresent, omnipotent and omniscient Self.

बन्ध मुद्रा

Bandha and Mudra

*Bandha means a tie, lock, knot, seal.
Mudras are neuro-muscular expressions.*

The ancient science of yoga uses bandhas to stimulate energy circuits in the body and the mind in order to access the deeper physical psychic and spiritual realms. Combined with pranayama, they, regulate the pranic energy and direct it safely to the higher brain centres.

The Mudras help to convey our thoughts more effectively. As attitudes of the body, they surpass language barriers and make communication easier and better. They are archetypal and are generally universally understood and accepted. We use the whole body, hands, facial expressions, eye movements etc, all the time in order to express ourselves more effectively. Common gestures are nodding the head, bowing down, smiling, shaking hands, greetings etc. To express anger or dislike, we sternly point the index finger or give an angry look. To stop somebody speaking, we place the index finger on the lips. In classical Indian dance, mudras play a big part. A performer portrays stories through facial expressions and through movements of hands, fingers, eyes and body.

Whole body mudras include Viparitkarni, Mahamudra and Yogamudra, whereas Jnana and Pranamudras are performed with hands only. Successful practice of bandhas and mudras increases physical and mental energy, interiorization and focus of the mind, calmness and clarity of thought, cessation of the breath. They are refreshing and rejuvenating.

Through specific asanas, pranayamas, bandhas, mudras, concentration, meditation and visualisation, a yogi exerts the required amount of focus and pressure on the chosen parts of the spine. This prevents the dissipation of bio-energies, stimulates the chakras and invokes, raises and guides the kundalini shakti (macrocosmic universal energy). Muscle constriction strongly forces afferent nervous impulses to move up to the brain to arouse various brain centres. At the same time, the awakened impulses that are coming down are restricted. This immense struggle alters the state of the practitioner's consciousness.

When the floodgates of man's store of potential energies are opened and safely channelled, man is led by his divine intuitive wisdom. He experiences and expresses divinity. His thoughts, speech and actions bring joy and peace to himself and to others. However, the awakening of kundalini shakti can be lethal if this vital energy is not handled wisely. If aroused with impure intent, it could cause nervous and physical exhaustion, premature decay, degeneration, disease and even death. Therefore, it is advised that before plunging into attempts to awaken kundalini, one ought intelligently and patiently to seek expert advice and supervision. It is important also to make sure that the vessel for housing and handling this vital energy is sound. One has to be physically, mentally and psychically strong and sturdy, and ready to handle the force of this power. Otherwise it would be like fitting a 100w bulb in a fitting that can only handle 40w. The obvious result would be that the fuse would blow.

N.B. When practising the following bandhas and mundras, where no specific breathing instructions have been given, please breathe normally.

Shaktisharini or Shaktchalanam Bandha

Shakti means energy
Sharini means moving
Chalanam means moving

Method
1) Sit firm, erect and relaxed in Padmasana (posture no.71).
2) Hold the feet with the hands. Breathe in, contracting the abdomen and anus in and up. Hold for a short comfortable period. Breathe out, relaxing the abdomen and anus. When the anus is contracted on inhalation, the apana impulse is stimulated to ascend, whereas the corresponding contraction of the abdomen generates the prana. This activity stimulates the Muladhara chakra, Svadhisthana chakra and Manipura chakra.

Khechari Mudra

Khech means pull
Ari means towards

Method
Sit comfortably tall and firm in a meditation posture. Close the mouth and inhale through the nose, roll the tongue back to the throat to reach the posterior nasal openings with the tip. The tongue rolled like this effectively prevents exhalation. Hold for a few comfortable seconds. Unroll the tongue and breathe out completely under control. Relax. Khechari draws the root of the tongue forward causing the expansion of the larynx, the closing of the glottis and the lifting up of the lower jaw. The mind easily focuses and relaxes.

Viparitkarni Mudra

Viparit means upside down, inverted.
Karni means act.

Method
1. Lie flat on the back.
2. Bend the legs and bring the thighs onto the abdomen. Press the palms firmly into the floor beside the hips and raise the hips, folded legs and the back off the floor. Place the palms on the buttocks and the elbows on the floor, to support the body. Straighten the legs keeping the back approximately at an angle of 45 degrees to the ground and the legs stretched at about 130 degrees to the trunk. Hold the hips firmly on the hands with the elbows fixed on the ground. Keep the chin slightly away from the chest to allow comfortable breathing.
3. Remain in posture, concentrating on the navel, throat and the breath for a comfortable period relaxing as much as possible.
4. On exhalation, either bend the knees to the forehead, slide the hands over the buttocks and lower the body to the floor without jerking the neck, or lower the hands to the floor and use them to control the body.
5. Relax.

Note

In Yoga, the fire or sun centre is at the navel whereas the moon centre, the cool centre is at the roof of the mouth (the palate). As opposed to the normal standing and sitting postures, in Viparitkarni the navel centre (fire) is high whereas the throat centre (lunar) is low.

Benefits

It alleviates circulatory problems in the legs as the blood flows easily to the heart and lungs and from there the fresh, oxygenated blood supply is increased to the neck and brain. The digestive system is helped to function better. It is an excellent mudra for varicose veins and piles. The posture induces quietness, stillness, creativity and care as the cooling, soothing effect of the moon is the base of this inverted pose. In this kriya, the energy (shakti) easily flows from the lower centres to the higher meditation centres in the brain.

Manduki
(Frog Seal)

Method

1. Sit erect yet relaxed in Padmasana (posture no.71), Siddhasana (posture no.70) or a comfortable meditation pose with the eyes closed.
2. Close the mouth but do not press the teeth. Consciously move the tip of the tongue slowly inside the mouth, touching and feeling all the parts of the mouth for a few seconds. Relax the tongue and keep the consciousness still in the mouth. Whilst practising Manduki, one may swallow the saliva if necessary. This simple mudra aids digestion and develops concentration and peace. It is very beneficial to practise this before a meal.

Sambhavi Mudra

Sama means even
Bhava means attitude

Method

1. Sit erect and still in Padmasana (posture no. 71) or a comfortable meditation posture.
2. Keep the eyes open and raise the gaze slightly up and fix it comfortably without blinking at the Ajna centre between the eyebrows for as long as you can. The mudra helps develop concentration, calmness, even-mindedness and many other beneficial attributes.

Ashvini Mudra

Ashva means horse.
Ini means the one that does.

Sitting in a comfortable pranayama posture, the sphincter muscle of the anus is contracted during a long, steady inhalation and is relaxed during a long steady exhalation. Practising; this continuously for a period without interruption awakens energy in the Muladhara and Swadhisthana chakras at the base of the spine in the perineum region. It helps develop focus. Horse like galloping movements of the mind are controlled by Ashvini.

Jalandhara Bandha

Jalan means web or net.
Adhara means base, support.

Method

1. Sit erect and comfortable in Padmasana (posture no.71), Sukhasana (posture no. 2) or any other comfortable meditation posture.
2. Breathe in slowly and steadily through both nostrils. At the end of the inhalation, practise a comfortable kumbhaka (retention). At the same time, contract the front of the neck and the throat and lower the head, bringing the chin down in between the collar-bones and at the top of the breast bone. Keep the spine upright and the back of the neck stretched. Fix the mind on the eyebrow centre. Hold the breath for a comfortable count.

3. Lift the chin and relax the bandha and exhale slowly and steadily. Let the normal breathing pattern establish itself. Relax before practising again.

Benefits
This bandha energises the throat, neck, chest, heart, respiratory organs and the spine. It also helps develop concentration. Freshness, control and calmness are felt. Practise a few times relaxing in between.

Mula Bandha

Mula means root, base, fundament.

Method
1. Sit firm erect and relaxed in Siddhasana (posture no.70).
2. Breathe in through both the nostrils lightly contracting and drawing in and up the sphincter muscle of the anus and the pelvic floor. Press in the centre of the perineum firmly with the heel of the right foot.
3. Hold the posture and the breath comfortably, for a few seconds. Exhale and relax the contraction simultaneously.
4. Relax and breathe normally.

Benefits
In the kumbhaka state, in order to cause the necessary restriction which will stimulate the muladhana, svadhisthana and the solar plexus, the seat and upright spine should be supported firmly by the ground, the heel should be pressed firmly into the centre of the perinium and the anus and lower abdomen should be contracted on inhalation.

Mula bandha tones the bladder, anus, rectum, large and small intestines. The whole abdominal area benefits from this exercise.

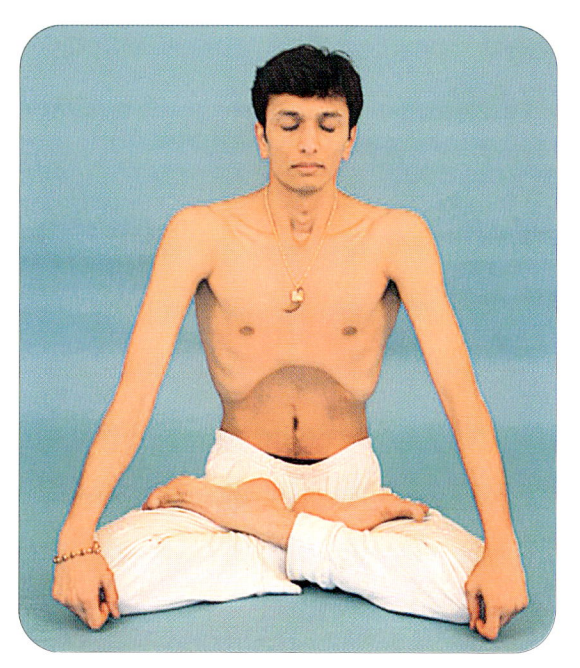

Uddiyana Bandha

Uddiyana means flying.

Method
1. Sit firm, erect and relaxed in Siddhasana (posture no.70) or any other pranayama posture.
2. Inhale slowly and steadily through the nostrils. Hold the breath for a comfortable period. Start exhaling steadily through the nostrils and at the end of exhalation hold the out-breath, pull in the entire abdominal area from the anus towards the spine, and up towards the sternum. Hold the bandha for a comfortable count.
3. Relax the bandha smoothly. Start inhaling steadily. Relax and let the renewed normal breathing rhythm settle down before practising again.

Benefits
It massages, strengthens and relaxes the abdominal organs. It relieves gas, constipation, flatulence and dyspepsia and develops concentration.

Maha Bandha

Maha means great.

When Mula, Jalandhara and Uddiyana are practised in one round of pranayama, it is called Maha Bandha.

Method
1. Sit firm, erect and relaxed in Siddhasana (posture no.70).
2. On inhalation, practise the Mula bandha. Hold the breath, implementing the Jalandhara bandha whilst; still holding the Mula bandha. Hold for a comfortable period.
3. Lift the head and relax the Jalandhara bandha. Exhale steadily with control, relaxing the Mula bandha slowly and smoothly. At the end of the complete exhalation, instead of instinctively breathing in again, practise the Uddiyana bandha. Hold for a comfortable period.
4. Relax the Uddiyana bandha smoothly and inhale deeply as in Ujjayi pranayama. Breathe out and relax before attempting to practise again.

This is one round of Maha Bandha.

Benefits
The benefits of all the three bandhas are experienced. It is most beneficial to practise Maha bandha before meditation as it prepares the body, mind and breath for concentration and meditation.

नाडी चक्र

Nadis and Chakras

It should be understood that the Nadis and Chakras are not aspects of the gross physical body, but rather of the subtle physical body (aura, formative force field or etheric counterpart) that envelops its gross counterpart. Many of their characteristics should be understood metaphorically rather than literally.

The nadis are tubular energy channels (meridians) and the chakras are energy coils. According to the tantric manuals there are 72,000 nadis, ten of which are the most important. Of these, the three principal ones are Ida, Pingala and Sushumna, Sushumna being in the centre. They are known to yogis as the astral spine.

Most texts on yoga say that the Ida nadi, associated with the moon, terminates at the left nostril and the Pingala nadi, associated with the sun, terminates at the right nostril. There are two different opinions regarding the course of the nadis through the subtle body. Some schools teach that ida is wholly on the left side and the pingala on the right side with the Sushumna supporting the chakras in the centre. This explanation corresponds with the ganglionated cords of the sympathetic nervous system which are situated on either side of the spinal column. Other schools teach that Ida and Pingala interlace in a double helix around the column of the Sushumna, and their intersections mark the position of the Chakras, the psychic energy centres. Sushumna starts from the kanda (the leaf shaped triangle with its apex pointed downward) below the Muladhara and runs up the vertebral column, dividing itself into an anterior turning, going to the forehead between the eyebrows at the root of the nose (Ajna chakra), and a posterior turning, going straight up behind the skull. This explanation of the Sushumna tallies with that of the spinal cord. At the base of the Sushumna in the centre of the Muladhara chakra lies dormant Kundalini shakti (cosmic energy).

A yogi's greatest achievement is to attain control of the Kundalini current and direct it according to his will. To do this, he first controls the functioning of the Ida and Pingala and the Panch Vayus (see chapter 'Pranayama') through pranayama, bandhas, mudras and meditations. With Kundalini power, a yogi can control the functioning of his vital organs and the wear and tear of the body and can prolong his life.

Energies at the lower three centres fulfil man's physical and material needs and ambitions. The higher three centres fulfil his creative and spiritual needs and desires. Many authors have compared chakras with the endocrine glands in the body although they are not at all the same.

There are seven major chakras. These are listed below together with their associated senses:

1. Muladhara   smell
2. Svadhisthana   taste
3. Manipuri   sight
4. Anahata   touch
5. Visudhi   hearing
6. Ajna
7. Sahasarara

There are also numerous minor ones.

1. Muladhara
(Knowledge of basic existence)
*Mula means the origin or the root.
It also means chief.
Adhara means the support or base.*

The position corresponds with earth plexus. It lies between the anus and the sex organs. Its description tallies accurately with that of the pelvic plexus. It is symbolised by a lotus with four petals in earthy red/brown colour. It is believed that in the centre of the Muladhara is the Kundalini Shakti lying dormant. When Kundalini is active it enables one to succeed in worldly ambitions. All the material and physical instincts and motivations in man are created and empowered by this centre. This chakra holds energy circuits leading to the lower abdominal organs, i.e. anus, rectum, bladder and reproductive organs. The bija (seed) sound that stimulates this chakra is 'Lang'.

The four individual petal sounds are Vang, Shang, Kshang and Sang.

2. Svadhisthana
(Seat of pure knowledge)
*Sva means self
Dhi means wisdom or clarity
Sthana means abode or place*

This chakra's tattwa (element) is water. Its base is at the tail bone and it tallies with the hypogastric plexus. It is symbolised by an orange coloured lotus with six petals. From here, the meridians bring energy to the reproductive organs, large and small intestines, rectum and bladder. With the focus on the sacral centre, one seeks to identify with one's true nature. One discovers the science of vibrational energy. One is less engrossed and less identified with the enveloping worldly consciousness. The bija sound to awaken this centre is 'Vang' and the six individual petal sounds are Bang, Bhang, Mang, Yang, Rang and Lang.

3. Manipura
(Abode of invaluable powers)
*Mani means an invaluable gem
Pura means abode or place*

This is the solar plexus located in the region of the navel. Its tattwa (element) is fire. It is symbolised by a ten petalled gold/orange/yellow fire coloured lotus. When Kundalini is vibrating at the Manipura we are vibrant with the warmth of love. We are tuned in with the self and able to receive and give love. We become intuitive, creative, understanding and sympathetic. We may develop psychic and clairvoyant powers. Physical strength in this centre is signalled by a strong physical constitution and a good digestion.

The bija sound that empowers this centre is 'Rang' and the ten petal sounds are Dang, Dhang, Rlang, Tang, Thang (palatals), Dang, Dhang (dental sounds), Nang, Pang, Phang (Labial sounds).

4. Anahata
(Seat of cosmic sound)
An means no or without • Hata means hitting

Here a meditating yogi hears the unbeaten sound of Brahma (AUM). This nerve centre is in the region of the cardiac plexus of the sympathetic nervous system. It is in the centre of the chest. The chakra is symbolised by a twelve petalled green lotus. Its tattwa (element) is air.

This nerve centre supplies energy to the chest, heart, lungs, aorta, and associated organs. Contemplation of this chakra develops love, compassion, understanding, joy and friendship. The more distant one is from this centre the more negative, unfulfilled and unhappy a person is. The bija sound to energise this centre is 'Yang', and the twelve petal sounds are Kang, Khang, Gang, Ghang, Yong, Cang, Chang, Jang, Jhang, Vang, Tang and Thang.

5. Visudhi
(Seat of Wisdom)
Vi means place. Sudhi means pure.

This is the pharyngeal plexus of the sympathetic nervous system based on the spine at the throat. It is symbolised by a lotus of sixteen petals in electric (etheric) blue. Its essence is akash (ether). The beneficial bija sound that invokes purity and clarity in one is 'Hang'.

When the vibrations here are strong, the words are clear, calm and sure, the speech is healing and inspiring and silently commands respect, love and even reverence. Effective contemplation on this centre purifies and rejuvenates the body and the mind through wisdom.

6. Ajna
(Seat of Authority)
It means loving command, Reverence.

Ajna chakra is an extension of the taluka (skull) chakra located in the cavernous plexus (medulla) and ending at the root of the nose between the eyebrows. It is also known as Param Triveni Padma (eternal lotus) bindu (spot) formed by the union of Ida, Pingala and the Sushumna nadis. It is the point focused upon during pranayama, prayers, dharana and dhyana. It is symbolised by a two petalled pure silver/white lotus. This is a Maha-tattwa centre.

This centre is active when the body, mind, senses and speech are in control. Strength at this centre enables one to give unconditional love. Peace and Joy are experienced in the presence of such a person. The eternal, omnipresent 'Aum' is the bija sound. The petal sounds, Hang and Kshang are used to invoke energy at the Ajna centre.

7. Sahasarara Padma
(Seat of Brahma)
Saha means together with.
Sarara means infinite.
Sahasarara means union with the Infinite.
Padma means lotus.

Sahasarara is located in the crown of the head. It is symbolised by a colourless/golden chakra. It is formless and at the same time its thousand petals are arranged in the form of an upside-down bell in rainbow colours. Its element is spirit. It is the seat of the supreme Bindu (spot).

This is where the journey of the consciously controlled kundalini of a yogi ends. When it is vibrating it is usually seen as a bright aura or light around the head and felt as the Presence. It is the silence and bliss seen on the face of a deeply meditating yogi. A yogi at this centre is a trikala jnani. He attains the wisdom of the entire universe. He is selfless in his motives, pure in his thinking, attitudes, behaviour and activities. He is an Avatar, a true Guru, a Paramahansa.

Kundalini

This is the static individualised microcosmic Shakti (energy) coiled up like a serpent in yog-nidra. It is resting above the kanda, in the centre of the Muladhara chakra. It has all the characteristics of the Wholeness of the cosmic energy. It has power to create and sustain everything. Supernatural miracles performed by yogis are due to this latent power awakened and converted into active energy. When willed to awaken from its slumber, Kundalini forces a passage through the Brahmanadi, stimulating the chakras into action as it rises to the crown of the head. The resurrection of the jivatman (soul) residing at the heart chakra becomes real. The most blissful, joyful union of Jiva Shakti (individualised soul energy) with Shivashakti (Spirit – macrocosmic energy) at Brahmadwara (the central point of the crown centre) takes place. All visions and Jnana (Knowledge) of the Universal Mind become available to the soul. An abundance of power, aligned to his natural characteristics comes to a yogi. Perception of the beauty and divinity of the Self showers his being with Bliss and Love, Wisdom and Joy. His soul, is at last free from the bondage of the body and mind. All the activities of body, mind, prana (breath), chitta (consciousness) and vasna (desires) are stilled and silenced as a yogi blissfully and joyfully dissolves into That.

सत्कर्म

Sat Karma

Sat means Good • Karma/kriya means Act

Sat Karma are cleansing and purifying techniques of yoga. They include four netis (Jala, Sutra or Catheter, Dugdha, and Ghrta), three dhoutis, (Kunjala or Gajkarni, Danda and Vastra), Nauli, Vasti, Tratakam and Shankhaprakshalana. They assist in the elimination of toxins and metabolic wastes from the system which otherwise may give rise to disease.

The cleansing kriyas, particularly the advanced ones, must be learnt under guidance. If practised wrongly, they could prove harmful. They must be practised in the morning after attending to the bladder and bowel and before breakfast. Relaxing after kriya is extremely important and most advisable.

When practising the following kriyas, if no specific breathing instructions have been given, please breathe normally. There are four Netis (washes).

1. Jala Neti

Jala means water. Neti means wash.
(A special jug is available for this kriya).

Take a sterilized neti jug or a pot with a spout that can hold approximately 100mls of water. The spout or the nozzle should be narrow enough (approximately 1/8 of an inch in diameter) to be easily inserted into the end of the nostril. Fill the jug with lukewarm water (boiled and cooled). Add a little salt. Let the salt completely dissolve in the water.

During the Jala neti one should keep the mouth slightly open and always breathe only through the mouth and relax as much as possible.

Method

Bend forward over the sink and hold the jug of water in the left hand. Tilt the head down to the right and slightly forward. Insert the spout into the lower end of the left nostril. Tilt and adjust the jug and the head to let the water start trickling in through the lower end of the left nostril. The water will pass up through the left nostril and start coming down and out through the right nostril in a thin stream. Initially the water may come out of the right nostril in drops or it may start flowing out from the same (left) nostril. Do not give up. With practice it will become easy. Remove the jug when it is empty, turn the face to the front and before you straighten up, gently blow and clean the nose properly to eliminate remains of dirt and water. Straighten up and relax. Repeat on the right nostril. Finish the kriya with some Bhastrika breaths (see pranayama) and some supine relaxation or meditation.

Benefits

The naso-pharyngeal passage is cleansed. The nostrils, throat and sinuses feel clearer. The air feels purer, lighter and cooler as though the quality of the air is changed. One feels light, calm and refreshed after this kriya. It is particularly good for treating a cold.

2. Sutra Neti or Catheter Neti

*Sutra means string or thread.
Neti means wash.*

Note: It is important to cut the finger nails and to wash the hands used in the kriya. This kriya is to be practised in front of a mirror. Keep the mouth slightly open throughout the practice, and breathe through the mouth only.

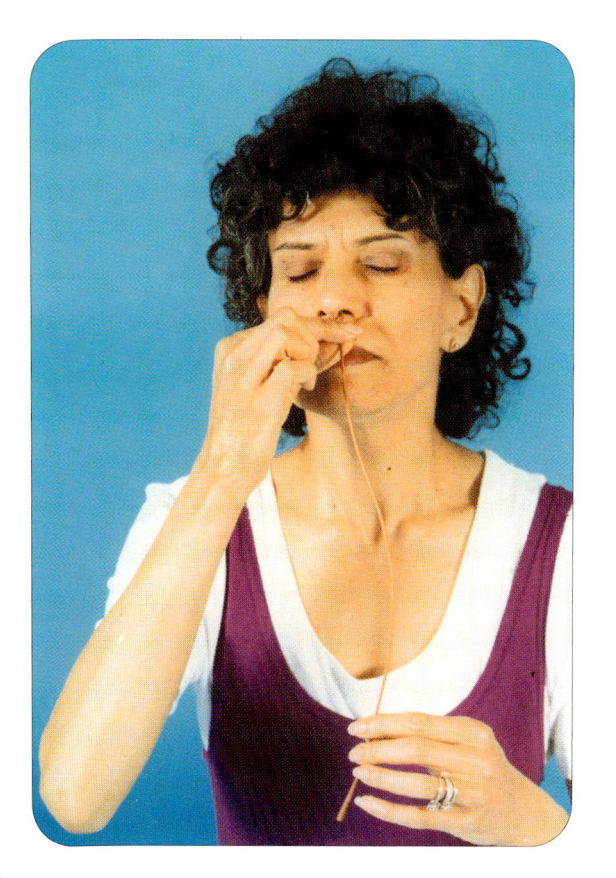

Method

Take a sterilised thin rubber tube about 1/8 of an inch in diameter and about twelve inches long. Introduce the tube gently into the left nostril with both the hands. Gently but firmly and confidently push this tube up the nostril until it is felt in the back of the throat. Open the mouth wider. Keep hold of the tube from outside with the left hand and reach into the throat and take hold of the other end of the tube with the index and the middle fingers of the right hand. Draw it half out of the mouth still holding the outer end with the left hand. Pull the tube carefully and gently up and down the naso-pharyngeal passage a few times with alternate hands; thus cleaning this passage between the nose and the throat. Gently but firmly and steadily pull the tube out through the mouth. Relax and rinse the mouth and blow the nose clean. Wash and sterilize the tube. Turn the head up and pour a few drops of ghee (clarified butter) or warm oil in the left nostril. Relax. Repeat by inserting the tube up the right nostril. Relax.

A beginner may feel irritation in the nostril on insertion of the tube and may want to pull the tube out and discontinue. When practised more often, the initial discomfort is not felt. However, if you feel a definite resistance when pushing the tube up the nostril, you should seek expert advice. Avoid this practice if you are unsure, when you have a cold or sore throat or if there is any bleeding as a result of this kriya. Traditionally only a string or thread was used for this practice.

Benefits

The naso-pharyngeal passage is cleansed. The nostrils, throat and sinuses are cleared and sensitized. The air feels finer, purer and cooler as if the quality of the air is changed. One feels light, calm and refreshed. The voice is calmer, clearer and sweeter.

3. Dugdha Neti
Dugdha means milk.

A neti pot with a spout about 1/8 of an inch in diameter and enough fresh milk kept at room temperature to fill the pot twice are required.

Method
Sit comfortably on a chair with the feet resting flat on the floor. Tilt the head up and open the mouth. With the neti pot gradually pour the milk up one nostril by inserting the spout of the pot in the lower end of the nostril. Close the opposite nostril with the index finger and let the milk trickle down the throat. This way as much milk as possible is taken in. When this is completed properly, release the opposite nostril, remove the spout, close the mouth, bend forward and blow the nose out and clean the nostrils. Relax and repeat on the other side.

This practice should be preceded by Jala neti and Bhastrika pranayama so as to make sure the nose and the pharyngeal passages are clean.

Benefits
The milk therapy soothes and heals the pharyngeal passages and nerves. The sinuses and head feel clear and the nervous system is soothed.

4. Ghrta Neti
Ghrta means ghee (clarified butter).
Neti means wash.

This is exactly the same as the Dugdha neti except that slightly warm ghee is used instead of the milk.

The naso pharyngeal passages are cleaned of dirt and mucous, and are oiled and greased properly. The nerves are toned, sensitized and soothed. For a period of time after the netis, the air one breathes feels light, cool and pure. The mind feels clear and calm. One feels refreshed and relaxed.

Dhouti
Dhouti means to wash

There are three types of Dhoutis

1. Kunjala or Gajkarni Dhouti.
2. Danda Dhouti
3. Vastra Dhouti

All the dhoutis must always be learnt under supervision and practised on an empty stomach first thing in the morning after attending to the bladder, and the bowel and before breakfast.

1. Kunjala or Gajkarni
The word Kunjal is derived from the word 'Kunjara' which means elephant.
The word Gaja also means elephant and karni means activity.

Note: Nails of the right hand must be cut properly and the hand thoroughly washed.

Just as an elephant sucks in and squirts the water out through its trunk, the water in this exercise is taken in and expelled through the mouth.

Method
Sit relaxed in a squatting posture on the floor. If this is difficult, you may sit comfortably on a chair. Drink as much warm salty water (one quarter of a teaspoon of salt to a litre of water) as you can, until no more can be taken. Stand up with feet hip-width apart and knees slightly bent. Bend forward from the hips. Put the right hand in the mouth and tickle the uvula with the middle and the index finger until the water starts coming out. Remove the hand and let the water flow out in a continuous stream. When the water stops, put the hand again in the mouth to tickle the uvula until all the water is out. At the end you will feel like vomiting as you tickle the uvula but no water comes out. This will mean that there is no more water in the stomach. Practise some Bhastrika breaths just to make sure. Relax in Shavasana (posture no. 1).

Benefits

Gajkarni brings about anti-peristalsis which throws the stomach content out. It exercises and stimulates the digestive organs. Any toxic food debris, excess mucus and bile are thrown out, giving a good stimulating wash to the oesophagus and stomach. One feels cleaner, calmer and lighter.

2. Danda Dhouti

Danda means tube.
Dhouti means wash.

A strong rubber tube about two and a half feet long and about half an inch in diameter is needed for this kriya. Make sure this tube is sterilised and the edges are smooth.

Method

Stand with the feet about one foot apart. Drink as much luke-warm water as you can until no more can be taken. Slightly bend forward from the hips, bend the knees and relax. Insert the tube into the mouth and throat with both hands. Firmly but gently and skilfully, send it down the oesophagus. As the tube descends to the stomach, the water already drunk will automatically start squirting out through the mouth. Ignore this, but carry on pushing the tube down gently and firmly until about two feet of the tube is swallowed. The remaining few inches of the tube is held outside the mouth with the hands.

Be patient and relax. Shake and move the tube gently. The water will start coming out in a steady stream through the tube as the anti-peristalsis of the stomach is brought about. Some water may start oozing out through the mouth too. As one practises more often, one feels less nervous and tense and the water will ooze out mainly through the tube in a constant flow, as from a tap. When the water stops coming out in spite of shaking and moving the tube, the tube should be slowly and gently drawn out. Some water may ooze out at the same time. Wash the mouth and do a few rounds of Bhastrika pranayama and then relax. This is a very difficult process and should never be attempted without expert guidance.

Benefits

Excess bile is removed making one feel cleaner, lighter and refreshed.

Danda dhouti energizes the digestive tract and stimulates digestive juices. Appetite improves and the food tastes better.

3. Vastra Dhouti

Vastra means cloth. Dhouti means clean.

A 20 feet long and 3 inches wide, soft, unbleached white muslin cloth is required for this kriya. The cloth should be sterilized and rolled up when slightly damp. Put the roll in a bowl of boiled, lukewarm water. Wash the hands thoroughly.

Method

Sit in Sukhasana (posture no. 2), or comfortably on a chair. Unroll the cloth slightly and put the loose end of the cloth to the back of the mouth with the thumb, index and middle fingers of the right hand keeping the roll in the bowl. Draw out the fingers keeping the cloth there. Pull the cloth up from the roll, a little at a time with your hands and slowly start swallowing it a little at a time, just as you would swallow food. In the beginning this may irritate and you may feel like vomiting and pulling the cloth out as it rubs against the tender mucous membrane lining of the throat. Relax and resist the temptation. In the beginning, about one to two feet of cloth should be swallowed and drawn out. With patience and practice the entire piece is swallowed keeping only a few inches in the left hand. Stand up and practise Nauli a few times. The cloth will absorb fluids and mucus in the stomach. After a few minutes the slippery cloth is drawn out gently, a little at a time with the hands and placed in the bowl. If any discomfort is felt on drawing it out, relax and swallow a few more inches again and then start pulling it out carefully and gently until all is out. Wash the mouth thoroughly, blow the nose and relax.

Benefits
Vastra Dhouti is excellent for relieving skin and chest disorders. It helps to remove toxins and excess kapha (phlegm) from the digestive tract. It stimulates and revitalizes the digestive system. One's appetite and digestion improves. One feels light and clean after it. A feeling of calmness and freshness lingers on for many many hours.

Nauli

Nauli means washing.

Nauli is an advanced exercise of the abdominal rectus muscles. In the beginning it must be learnt and practised under supervision.

Method
Stand with the feet about two feet apart. Bend the knees and the trunk forward a little. Place the hands on the thighs just above the knees. Relax and watch the breath. After a complete exhalation, instead of breathing in, draw the abdominal muscles in and up so that a hollow is formed in the abdomen. Still holding on to this hollow and the out-breath, force the rectus abdomini to stand out like a ridge. Hold the breath and the ridge for a few comfortable seconds. Relax the abdominal muscles gently and then breathe in deeply and steadily. Relax and let the breath and the body get used to its renewed rhythm.

With practice the rectus abdomini stands out properly. Once control is attained on rectus abdomini, alternatively contract and relax the muscles a few times at a stretch still holding onto the out-breath comfortably.

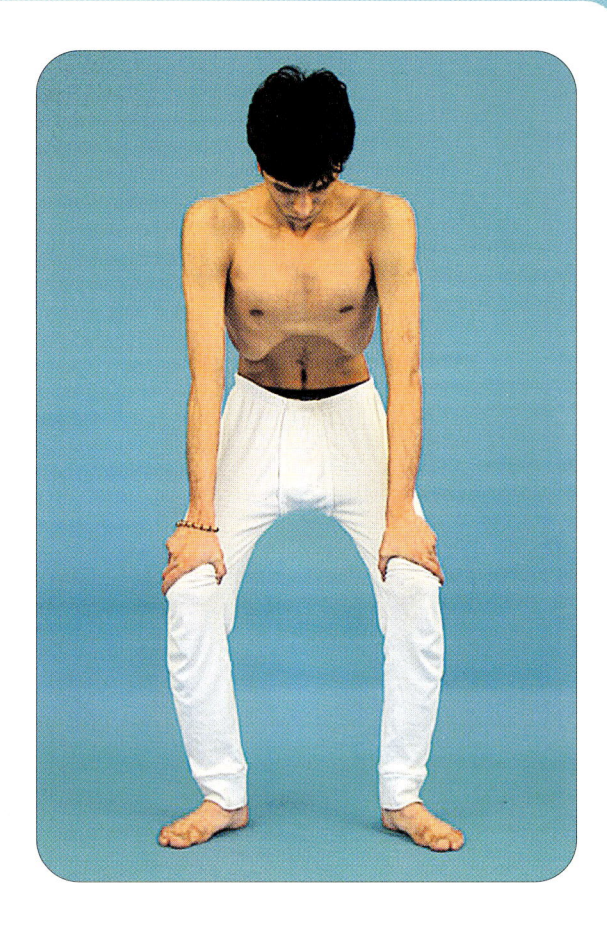

Vama-Dakshina Nauli
Method
This may be practised by advanced nauli practitioners by leaning to the left and moving the nauli to the left and by leaning to the right and moving the ridge to the right. Once the rectus abdomini muscles are moved easily to the left and to the right, then one can learn to rotate them.

Benefits
Nauli stimulates the digestive metabolism by increasing peristaltic movements. Nauli can powerfully contract and relax the abdominal viscerae and is thus the most effective way of exercising the abdominal organs deeply and releasing deep tensions and toxins from the abdominal organs. It relieves gas and constipation and revitalizes abdominal organs. It improves the appetite and the processes of digestion, assimilation and elimination. It strengthens the body's immune system. It improves the workings of the diaphragm, lungs, ribcage and heart.

Vasti

A sterilized eight inch long, strong plastic tube or rubber hose, about a quarter to a half inch in diameter is required.

Method
Fill the bath with purified warm water up to the navel. Smear for a few inches the end of the tube/hose with castor oil, and gently insert it in the anus. Push the tube up gently, leaving about one to one and a half inches out. Sit in the squatting posture in the bath. On inhalation, contract and hold the lower abdominal and anus muscles in and up. At the same time, draw the water up through the anus. This process will continue until the hold is relaxed. When sufficient water is sucked in, relax the abdomen, breathe normally and remove the tube gently still holding the drawn water in the colon. Stand up and practice Nauli i.e. simple, vama, dakshina or rotation, according to your ability. This movement will swirl and shake the water in the colon cleaning it thoroughly in the nooks, crannies, and corners. Sit on the toilet and expel the contents in the normal way. After repeating this process a few times, clear water will come out, indicating a thoroughly cleansed bowel. Relax in Shavasana (posture no. l).

Benefits
Vasti relieves one of intestinal disorders and tones the bowel particularly the rectum and anus. It cleans old debris, toxins and gas from the colon giving it a good rejuvenating wash. Constipation is relieved. A lot of blocked energy is freed in the process. One's digestion, assimilation and elimination processes improve and one feels full of vitality and bounce.

Mayurasana (posture no. 86) after the vasti is highly recommended. It must also be learnt under guidance.

These days, to clean the colon, either enemas or colonic irrigations are applied which are easy and less messy, although not quite so natural and effective.

Tratakam

The two popular objects used for Tratakam are:
1. A small black paper disc
2. A candle.

Method
Place a burning candle, in a dark room, at about arm's length and at eye level . Take Padmasana (posture no.71), or Sukhasana (posture no 2), or sit firm, erect and relaxed on a chair. Stare at the light of the candle without blinking. Gradually open the eyes wider and keep the gaze fixed. This will focus the mind and counteract the tendency to blink.

After a few seconds relax the gaze, but keep them focused all the time on the candle-light till the tears start to flow. Close the eyes and let them relax for a few minutes, letting the tears flow naturally. Open them, blink and relax.

Benefits
This exercise increases alertness and concentration. It washes the eyes ridding them of sticky toxins. It stimulates life force in and around the eyes and nerves, thus, strengthening the eye muscles, improving the eyesight and the functioning of the nervous system. A feeling of well-being, calmness, strength and freshness is experienced.

N.B. Epileptics should not practise with a candle flame.

Shankhaprakshalana

Shankha means conch.
Prakshalana means moving through.

The conch-shaped passage of the digestive tract from the mouth through to the stomach and intestines gives the name to this cleansing process. The process must be learnt under guidance. It takes 3 to 4 hours. One must keep oneself warm during the practice. It is advisable to eat lightly the day before.

Shankhaprakshalana is to be practised early in the morning, after attending to the bladder and the bowel and before breakfast.

Prepare 16 to 18 glasses of lukewarm saline

water (approx. 1/4 tsp of salt per litre of boiled lukewarm water). Learn the five asanas shown on the previous two pages.

Method
Drink two glasses of water. Perform the five asanas eight times each in the order listed (ref. to page 167 and 168).

Again drink two more glasses of water and perform the set of asanas eight times each. In between this programme you may, if you feel like it, evacuate the bowel or pass urine. At first some solid stools and then some semi-solid stools, watery stools, and finally clear water will be evacuated signifying a clean bowel. It is advisable to go and sit on the toilet after six glasses of water, even if you do not feel like it. Each individual body responds differently, so give yourself time. Lashoo Shankha (short wash) finishes after six glasses of water.

The quantity of water consumed may vary from individual to individual. Although 16 to 18 glasses is the average, up to 25 glasses could be taken in full Shankha. When you have finished the practice, lubricate the anus with a little ghee (clarified butter) or vegetable oil.

Practice of Kunjala Dhouti after the Shankhaprakshalana is of great benefit.

Relax for about an hour in Shavasana (posture no. 1). A meal of rice and lentils cooked together (khichdi) with clarified butter is consumed after relaxation. This lubricates and activates the systems. One must eat as simple and as pure a diet as possible for at least three weeks after the full Shankha. Heavy to digest foods may give rise to discomfort. A light diet of well cooked organic vegetables, fruits and easy to digest grains and lentils is recommended. Meat, acidic foods like lemons, oranges and pineapples, spices and dairy produce (except the ghee, in small amounts) should be avoided. Coffee, alcohol, cigarettes etc are restricted during these weeks. All the steps and rules of the kriya must be adhered to strictly. It is most advisable not to attempt full Shankha without expert supervision.

For Lashoo Shankha (short wash), dietary restrictions are not necessary although a meal of khichdi and ghee after the wash is a good idea.

Benefits
By this technique, the digestive tract is cleaned and freed of old debris, toxins and metabolic wastes. It gives rest to the digestive system and balances its functioning and movements. It improves digestion, assimilation and elimination. It also sensitizes the taste buds and normalizes appetite. One feels light, refreshed and revitalized.

The energy-flow along the tract is properly re-established. The chakras are stimulated and their functions are harmoniously balanced in the process. One feels physically, mentally and emotionally clean and clear.

Since the root of most diseases can be traced to toxicity of the colon, this cleansing process helps most conditions. It should never be attempted without expert supervision.

Shankha is good for constipation, gas, acidity, indigestion, bladder/kidney infections, diabetes etc. It is not recommended for people suffering from duodenal or colon ulcers or any debilitating diseases. High blood pressure sufferers should avoid salt.

Asana to practise:

1. Utthita Tadasana • **2.** Tiryaka Tadasana • **3.** Kati Chakrasana • **4.** Tiryaka Bhujangasana
5. Udarakarshanasana.

Note: Breath control is not necessary,

**Utthita means extended.
Tada means mountain.**

1 **Utthita Tadasana**: Stand with the feet hip width apart. Interlock the hands in the front. On inhalation, turn the palms up and stretch the arms above the head raising the body on the toes. Stretch fully and hold for a second or two. On exhalation, lower the heels and arms.

Practise eight times and go on to number 2.

**Tiryaka means side.
Tada means mountain.**

2 **Tiryaka Tadasana:** Stand with the feet hip width apart. Interlock the hands in the front. Inhaling, turn the palms up, stretch the arms above the head raising the feet on the toes. Exhaling, bend to the right. Inhaling, stretch back to the centre and exhaling bend to the left. Inhaling, stretch back to the centre. Remain on the toes and practise the side bends eight times, alternatively on each side. After the last time, when in the centre, exhaling, lower the arms and heels and go on to number 3.

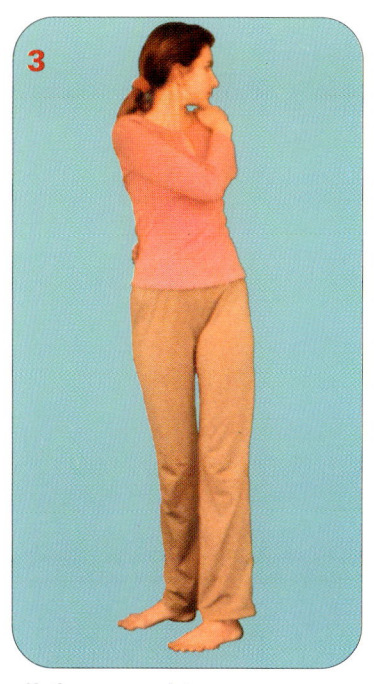

**Kati means waist.
Chakra means twist.**

3 **Kati Chakrasana**: Stand with the feet hip-width apart. Exhaling, twist the trunk to the left, turn the head to look back over the left shoulder. At the same time, put the right hand on the left shoulder and swing the left arm back to the right side of the waist. Breathing in, return to the centre and repeat on the opposite side with the opposite arms. Practise eight times alternatively on each side. After the last time, when in the centre, lower the arms and bring the feet together. Go on to number 4.

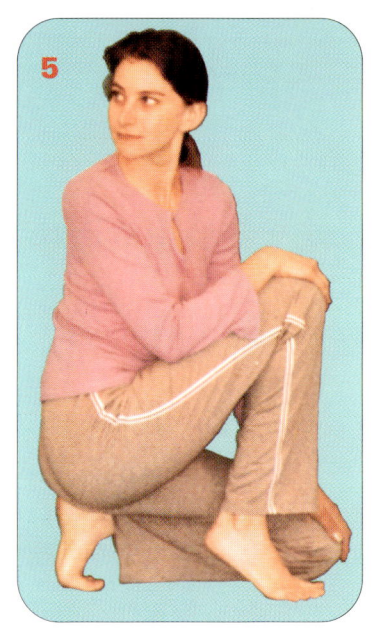

**Tiryaka means side.
Bhujanga means cobra.**

**Udar means stomach.
Karshana means pull/press.**

4 Tiryaka Bhujanasana: Lie face down with the feet apart, toes tucked under, and the palms flat on the floor near the shoulders. Place the chin on the floor and inhaling, raise the trunk up by pressing the palms into the floor in Bhujangasana (Posture no.25). Twist the trunk and head to the left and look back at the feet. Untwist and come back to the centre. Stay in the cobra posture and repeat on the right side. Practise eight times on each side. After the last time when in the centre, exhaling, lower the trunk and head. Go on to number 5.

5 Udara Karshanasana: Squat with the feet approximately 10 inch apart and the hands cupping the knees. Lower the left knee to the ground and bring it as near to the right foot as possible. Rest the left buttock on the left foot with the toes tucked in.

Exhaling, twist the body and the neck to the right. At the same time with the right hand, push the right thigh against the abdomen. Come back to the starting squat position. Now lower the right knee to the ground and bring it as near to the left foot as possible. Rest the right buttock on the right foot with the toes tucked in. Exhaling, twist the body and the neck to the left. At the same time, with the left hand push the left thigh against the abdomen. Practise alternatively eight times on each side. After the last time, when in the centre, stand up and start again from asana no. 1 (Utthita Tadasana) and continue until all the water is finished.

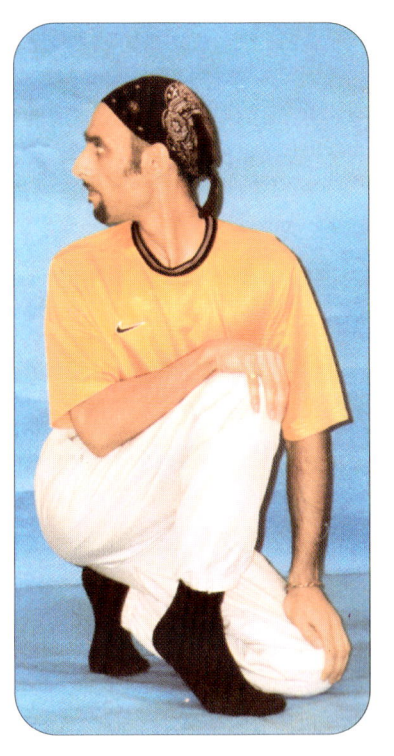

168

योग

Yoga Therapy

Yoga teaches us that we are responsible for our actions and we must always remember that every action brings a consequence. We have a choice either to cultivate positive thinking and carry out right actions and enjoy the fruits of material and spiritual wealth or suffer the consequences of bad actions. If we sow the right seeds we are bound to reap success as Galatians 6:7 says "Whatsoever a man soweth, that shall he also reap."

In order to use yoga successfully for therapeutic purposes, it is important to understand the vastness, multiple uses and priceless benefits of this science. With sound knowledge and understanding of the human body and mind, and with discipline, everybody, whether lay-people or professionals, can use yoga to treat ailments and afflictions.

A yoga therapist first assesses the patient's condition and then plans suitable yoga treatment sessions for him. These include:
1. Asana (yoga postures)
2. Pranayama (breathing techniques)
3. Sat-kriyas (cleansing techniques)
4. Bandhas and mudras (locks and gestures)
5. Diet and nutrition
6. Yog-nidra (relaxation)
7. Dhyana (meditation)
8. Jnana (knowledge).

The patient must follow the prescribed routine strictly, as directed. Any adjustments necessary are made in the consultations which follow. The length of the treatment depends on the nature of the illness, the patient's age, the regularity and the quality of the discipline with which the patient follows the given programme. The patient's awareness of and relationship with body, soul and higher Self is important.

Yoga teaches us that we are beings with many facets: physical, social, emotional, intellectual and spiritual. All these are interdependent and should be developed fully. If one aspect is weak or missing the person suffers.

The facets of a personality are referred to as Koshas.

1. Annamaya kosha
This is the glossy layer we call physical, and the one of which we are most aware. We identify closely with our body – a priceless possession to which we remain deeply attached. It is mainly sustained by the prana and energy in anna (food). It can be rendered healthy by good eating habits, a simple life-style and by ashtanga – asana, pranayama, sat kriya, yog-nidra and meditation.

2. Pranamaya kosha
The principal feature of this second layer is life force (prana). Through pranayama, a yogi masters his breath, and in turn his life force. He becomes the controller of his life. Just like Annamaya (physical) kosha, Pranamaya (breath) layer can be kept healthy by following good eating habits, a simple lifestyle and practice of

ashtanga, particularly asana, pranayama, sat-kriya (cleansing acts), yog-nidra and meditation.

3. Manomaya kosha
This is a more subtle layer we know as mind. It can be developed by keeping good company, studying the scriptures and following the teachings of one's Guru. The state of mind is directly affected by Anna and Prana koshas and they are affected by Manomaya kosha.

4. Vijnanamaya kosha
Vijnanamaya (wisdom), the fourth layer, refers to the buddhi tattwa (i.e. element of discriminative knowledge and intelligence). This is the realm of understanding, intuition, insight and creative ability. Tuned in to this level, a yogi is able to see clearly the true picture of life. He is able to discern and decide his course.

5. Anandamaya kosha
The fifth layer refers to Bliss – a state where a yogi is in tune with the Divine.

Through yoga one can regulate the breath and the workings of one's body and mind. One can keep oneself physically, mentally and spiritually in peak condition. It would be a serious misconception to consider yoga as just another physical training programme. Yoga is a science of Self. It helps one to achieve a fit and healthy body and mind and it transforms one's consciousness. If properly understood and practised, it is capable of giving us freedom from suffering.

If we identify with the body and direct our energies towards the acquisition of material possessions, we cannot make spiritual progress. In spite of our material well-being, we are often left with feelings of low self-worth and a vague half-recognized hunger for something of true value. When we recognize that the precious commodity we seek is our progress on a spiritual path, and when we tentatively take the first steps on that path, then, and only then will we experience joy, peace and fulfillment. We should say no to greed, selfishness and aggressive competition.

Those who succumb to the temptations of material desires may suffer stress which could result in psychosomatic illness.

While medicines have a role to play in the healing process, it is the individual who, recognising his true nature, will be able to cure himself successfully.

Yoga is the key to freedom from the stress of everyday existence many of us experience. It is a discipline which was almost lost but which has been revived in answer to mankind's most pressing need for spiritual enlightenment. Yoga is a skilful and dynamic discipline which helps de-toxify the mind and body, and makes one aware of one's responsibilities to oneself. Just as yoga helps to attain health and happiness, so a harmonious healthy way of living is beneficial and enhances one's progress in yoga. It is no wonder that this art – or call it a science – of the body, mind and soul has great appeal for all, regardless of age, creed, colour, race or religion.

Yoga begins with the disciplines of yama, niyama, asana, pranayama, pratyahara, dharana and dhyana, and leads to the freedom and joy of 'Samadhi'.

1. Asana Therapy
In this therapy the body is held firmly and comfortably in the posture and the mind is focused on the posture and the breath. The breath is allowed to flow freely or is guided to energise the body and mind. This causes movements and pressures in the chakra system along the spine, accessing the spiritual realm specific to the particular asana. Physical, psychological and spiritual blockages are cleared. The skeletal and muscular adjustments and alignments that occur enable the energy to flow throughout the body and all the systems are improved. The body and mind experience a change of focus and one gets relief from negative and repetitive thoughts. The natural harmony and felicitous rhythm of body and mind are re-established. Vitality, calmness, control and well-being are some of the many benefits one can expect. (*For more on asana therapy see the 'Asana'*).

2. Prana Therapy
The patient is taught breath control to foster good health.

If breath is	If breath is
Steady	Irregular
Quiet	Disturbed
Deep	Shallow
Long	Rapid

The result is	The result is
Health	Ill-health
Contentment	Stress
Peace of mind	Anger

Competitive physical exercises put unnatural pressure on the body and mind. As the emotions and thoughts affect the breath and energy levels, the regulation of breath corrects emotions and thoughts releasing energies for self-healing.

The extra oxygen intake in Prana Therapy oxygenates the blood and changes the vitality level and mood. Energy previously spent in dealing with toxicity is now used to improve the functioning of the body. Pranayama aerates, strengthens and relaxes the respiratory system including the muscles and the nerves. This helps to strengthen the body's defences.

Bandhas (locks) and mudras (gestures) applied in pranayama, awaken the energy in the spine which then flows to the brain and other parts of the body. This energy is useful for self-study and introspection. (*For more on Prana Therapy see 'Pranayama'.*)

3. Sat-Kriya (*see chapter on Sat-kriya*)

4. Bandhas and Mudras (*see chapter on Bandhas and mudras*)

5. Diet
According to the Ayurveda (knowledge of life), the food one eats should be for physical, mental and spiritual health and not just for taste and convenience.

One should have a balanced diet which includes organically grown fresh fruits, vegetables (both raw and cooked), sprouted grains, pulses, beans, nuts and seeds, low fat yoghurts, low fat cottage cheeses, suitable herbs and spices, and natural sweeteners i.e. honey, molasses etc. .

A sensible and nutritious diet means less drain on energy used in digestion, assimilation and elimination processes.

In the sixth chapter of Bhagavad Gita (VI:16-17), Krishna talks of moderation. He says that those who are moderate in all their actions, work and recreation, suffer less sorrow (or avoid sorrow). He says one should not overeat or fast unnecessarily.

Our diet affects our moods and our personality, and therefore, Krishna advises a diet which is not bland or highly flavoured, not too dry or too juicy, not too cold or too hot. Sattvic food is pure and non-irritant. It is rich in prana. It strengthens body and mind. It fosters good health and vitality and prolongs life. Tamasic food is devoid of life. It is impure. It breeds negative emotions and thoughts. It fosters ill-health. Rajasic food is hot, pungent and high in fat and protein. It may produce feelings of over-sensivity and aggression. Physical and mental disorders can result from over-indulgence in this type of food. The old saying 'We are what we eat' should be remembered. A balanced vegetarian diet harmonizes the functioning of the body and mind and creates peaceful thoughts and emotions.

Balanced meals suitable for individual needs, should be taken at regular intervals and when hungry.

Food, hygienically prepared with love and care should first be offered to God for blessing before it is consumed. Food should be well chewed to mix properly with saliva and should be eaten in silence.

6. Yog-Nidra Therapy (Relaxation)
After the practice of asana and pranayama, one relaxes in yoga's supine Shavasana (posture No. 1). The energy wasted by unnecessary movements of body, thoughts and emotions is minimized through the practice of Shavasana. All the energy awakened and/or tapped from asana and pranayama flow effectively throughout the body and mind. In Shavasana, the body and mind are saying, "We have done our best and now surrender to the will of nature. Right relaxation in the correct posture produces vital energy which reaches deeper levels in the body and mind. This also helps breathing which becomes regular and rhythmic.

A sense of well-being, freedom, peace and clarity of thought are just a few of the many benefits that are attainable through the practice of this humble, yet powerfully effective posture of yoga.

Visualisation, auto-suggestion and positive affirmation can be used during Shavasana to enhance the well being of the whole person.

7. Dhyana Therapy (Concentration and meditation therapy)

It is difficult to understand, unless experienced, that something so simple and easy can give so much well being and happiness in such a short time. No wonder the simple yet superb healing power of meditation is becoming an indispensable part of life for many in every corner of the globe. We all desire clarity, happiness, wisdom, strength and peace and these can be obtained by meditation. We come to know and understand our true selves and our purpose in life.

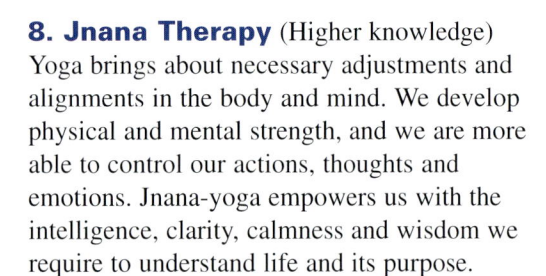

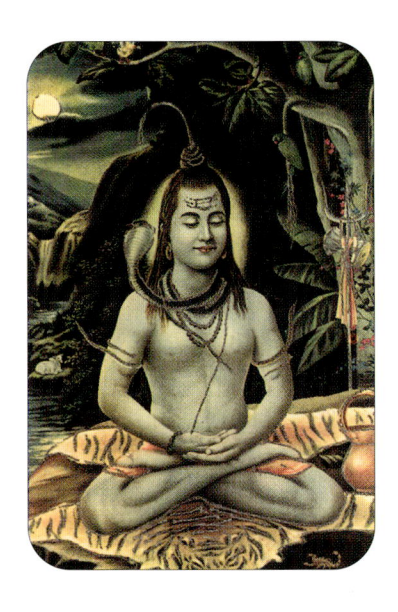

8. Jnana Therapy (Higher knowledge)
Yoga brings about necessary adjustments and alignments in the body and mind. We develop physical and mental strength, and we are more able to control our actions, thoughts and emotions. Jnana-yoga empowers us with the intelligence, clarity, calmness and wisdom we require to understand life and its purpose.

Glossary

Agarbha: Kumbhaka practised without a mantra

Ahimsa: Abstinence from cruelty

Ajna: The chakra between the eyebrows

Anahata: The heart chakra

Anandamaya kosha: Attunement with the divine joy

Annamaya kosha: The physical layer of existence – the body

Antara: Suspension of breath at the end of puraka

Apana vayu: Life-force of the lower abdomen

Aparigraha: Abstinence from greed

Asana: Posture

Ashtanga: Ashta – eight, anga – limb

Asteya: Abstinence from dishonesty

Atman: The soul

AUM (OM): Cosmic creative vibration

Bahir: Outer

Bahiya: Suspension of breath at the end of rechaka

Bandha: A tie, knot, seal, lock

Bang: A chakra sound

Bhagavad Gita: The Holy book of the Hindu religion

Bhakta: An instinctive devotee

Bhang: A chakra sound

Bija: A seed

Brahmacharya: Brahma – all-pervading spirit, Creator; acharya – guru

Brahmadwara: The central point of the crown centre; dwara – a door to the spirit

Brahmanadi: A principal nadi through which kundalini ascends

Buddhi tattwa: Element of discriminative knowledge and intelligent understanding

Chakra: Coiled energy

Chandra: The moon

Chang: A chakra sound

Dakshina Nauli: An advanced form of nauli

Danda: A tube, a rod/staff

Dang: A chakra sound

Dhang: A chakra sound

Dharana: Concentrated thought, reflection

Dhouti: To wash

Dhyana: Deep meditation, contemplation

Dugdha: Milk

Gang: A chakra sound

Ghang: A chakra sound

Ghrta: Ghee, clarified butter

Hang: A chakra sound

Hasta: Hands

Hatha Pradipika: Authoritative text of Hatha Yoga

Hatha Yoga: A type of yoga

Himsa: Violence

Ida: A principal nadi
Ishwar-Pranidhana: Total faith in God
Jala: Water
Jang: A chakra sound
Jhang: A chakra sound
Jiva: Self
Jiva Shakti: Microcosmic energy
Jivatman: Soul
Jnana: Knowledge of yoga
Kanda: Triangle on muladhara chakra
Kang: A chakra sound
Karma: The law of cause and effect
Karni: Activity
Khang: A chakra sound
Koshas: Layers, sheaths
Kriya: Activity
Kshang: A chakra sound
Kumbhaka: Suspension of breath
Kundalini: Cosmic energy
Kutastha: Energy centre between the eyebrows
Lang: A chakra sound
Linga Yoga: To link; to unite
Maha: Great
Maha-bharatha: Spiritual conflict
Mahatattwa: Complete element
Mandala: Geometric pattern
Mang: A chakra sound
Manipuri: The navel chakra
Manomaya kosha: The mind layer of existence
Mantra: Soul liberating sound
Maya: Illusion
Meru danda: The spinal column
Mudras: Neuro-muscular expressions; a symbol

Mukta: Release
Mulabandha: A bandha at the root chakra
Muladhara: The root chakra
Nadi Shudhana: A pranayama method; nadi – channel; shudhana – cleansing
Nadis: Tubular energy channels
Namaskara: Salutation
Nang: A chakra sound
Nauli: Washing
Neti: A wash
Nirbhikalpa: Total absorption
Nirbija: Pranayama practised without a mantra
Niyama: Positive resolutions
Pada: Feet, legs
Padam: Feet
Padma: Lotus
Panch vayus: The five life-forces activated by pranayama
Pang: A chakra sound
Paramahansa: A pure spirit
Paramatman: Holy Spirit
Phang: A chakra sound
Pingala: A principal nadi
Prana vayu: Life-force of the thorax and brain
Pranamaya kosha: The breath layer of existence
Pranava: The soul-liberating 'OM' sound
Pranayama: Prana – life; yama – control; breathing techniques
Pratyahara: Pratya – towards; hata – moving
Puraka: Inhalation, to fill up
Purana: Ancient Hindu text
Raja Yoga: The science of Self-realization
Rajasic (food): Over-stimulating food
Rang: A chakra sound

Rechaka: Exhalation, to bring out

Rishi: A seer

Rlang: A chakra sound

Sabija: Pranayama practised with a mantra

Sadhaka: A spiritual aspirant

Sagarbha: Kumbhaka practised with a mantra

Sahasarara: The crown chakra

Samadhi: Sama – balanced; adhi – state of consciousness

Samana vayu: Life-force of digestion at the navel centre

Samavritta: Equal duration of inhalation and exhalation

Samaya: Time and space

Samsara: Creation

Samskaras: Character-forming habits

Sang: A chakra sound

Santosha: Contentment

Sat: Truth

Satkriya: Cleansing techniques

Sattvic (food): Pure food, beneficial to health

Satya: Truth

Satyagrahi: Truth seeker

Satyuga: The golden age

Saucha: Purity

Shakti: Energy

Shang: A chakra sound

Shankhaprakshalana: A cleansing act; shankha – conch; prakshalana – moving through

Shanti: Peace

Shiva: The higher Self

Shivashakti: Macrocosmic energy

Steya: Dishonesty

Sushumna: A principal nadi

Sutra: A string, a thread, an aphorism

Svadhisthana: The sacral chakra

Swadhyaya: The study of self including the higher Self

Tamasic (food): Dead, putrid, harmful

Tang: A chakra sound

Tapa: To burn, to become hot

Tapasvi: One who is inflamed with the desire to search for truth

Tha: Moon

Thang: A chakra sound

Tratakam: A form of concentration

Triveni: Meeting point of three nadis

Udana vayu: Life-force controlling food and air intake

Vama Nauli: An advanced form of nauli

Vang: A chakra sound

Vasti: A cleansing act

Vastra: A cloth

Vijnanamaya: The kosha of wisdom, intuition, insight

Visudhi: The throat chakra

Vyana vayu: Life-force distributing energy throughout the body

Yama: Rules of morality

Yang: A chakra sound

Yog: Union

Yoga-sadhana: Discipline

Yognidra: Relaxation

Yong: A chakra sound

NOTES

NOTES

NOTES

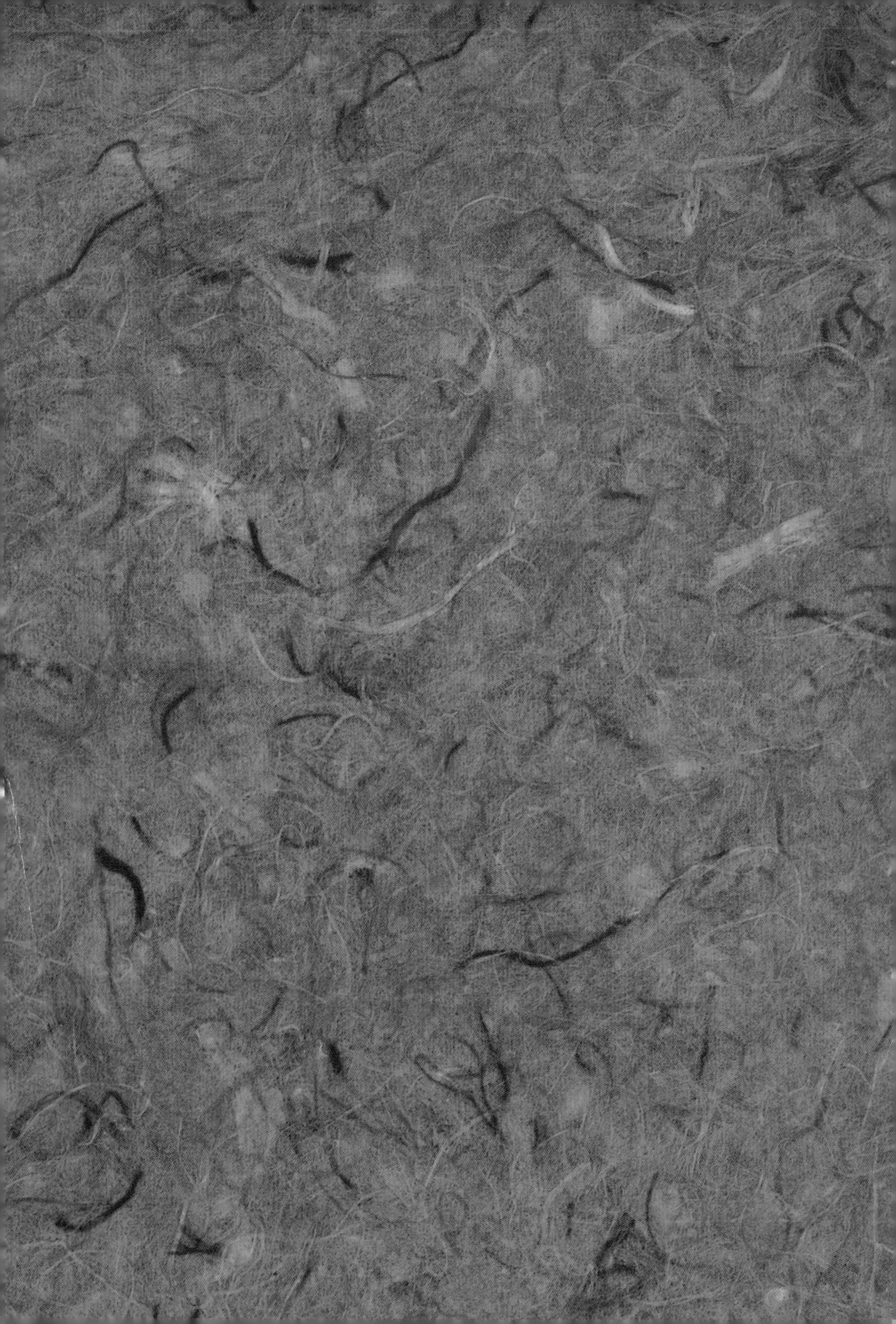